TAKE IT OFF AND KEEP IT OFF

For people who find salad without dressing unbearable . . . eggs without bacon unthinkable
. . . dinner without a martini uncivilized . . .

For people who think they must sacrifice rich
ice cream for watery sherbet . . . For those who
think the only diet is a painful diet . . . For
those who have yo-yoed from one rigid regimen
to another . . .

HERE AT LAST IS THE DIET FOR YOU.

It's simple, safe, and effective. And you call the
shots, plan the menus. Now you can eat happy
and grow slim on 60 carbohydrate grams a
day. And here's the easy, instant-reference
guide that makes low-gram living a snap and
a pleasure.

THE NEW
CARBOHYDRATE
GRAM COUNTER

Compiled by
MARGARET SULLIVAN

Totally revised
and updated

A DELL BOOK

Published by
Dell Publishing Co., Inc.
1 Dag Hammarskjold Plaza
New York, New York 10017

Dell ® TM 681510, Dell Publishing Co., Inc.

ISBN: 0-440-16311-0

Printed in the United States of America
First printing—February 1980
Second printing—October 1980

CONTENTS

THE NEW CARBOHYDRATE GRAM COUNTER

THE DIET FOR PEOPLE WHO HATE TO DIET

Are you overweight but unable to face the prospect of the usual dreary diet: celery stalks, carrot strips, and cucumber slices; skim milk, black coffee, and sauerkraut juice? If your answer is yes, then the low-carbohydrate diet is meant especially for you—for people who despise dieting, who find salad without dressing unbearable, eggs without bacon unthinkable, dinner without a martini uncivilized!

The low-carbohydrate diet permits you to eat as much protein and fat as you please. All you need to watch is your intake of carbohydrates—sugars and starches. Forget about calories. On this diet, you count carbohydrate grams; you limit your intake of carbohydrates to 60 grams daily. It's as simple as that—and almost as pleasant as not dieting at all! Mayonnaise and hollandaise, sour cream and heavy cream, a thick slice of ham, a rich leg of lamb—these and dozens of other usually "forbidden" foods are yours on the low-carbohydrate diet!

How can such a delightful diet work? In simplified form, here is the explanation. The energy your body needs to function is supplied largely by carbohydrates and fats (the main function of proteins is to rebuild tissue). Studies indicate that excessive consumption of carbohydrates is the primary cause of overweight. In other words, when your body doesn't burn up all the sugars and starches you eat, the excess carbohydrates turn quickly into unwelcome pounds. On a low-carbohydrate diet, your body is forced to call upon its own reserves of fat—stored-up carbohydrates—for energy; thus, you lose weight. Another reason for the success of the low-carbohydrate diet is that proteins and fats "stick to the ribs" (remain in the stomach) longer than sugars and starches; therefore, you're not perpetually hungry. Some scientists argue that a low-carbohydrate diet results in an intake of fewer calories, which in turn results in a loss of weight. Unquestionably, many low-carbohydrate dieters cut down on calories by drastically limiting their consumptions of foods such as cake, candy, bread, potatoes, pasta, etc. However, there are cases of dieters who have shed pounds while enjoying high-calorie, low-carbohydrate meals. Science still has much to learn about body chemistry and food, but this much at least is certain: Calories alone do not account for weight loss and gain. Nutritionists and other scientists may not always agree why a low-carbohydrate diet works, but there is general agreement that it does work!

What can you eat on a low-carbohydrate diet? Unlimited amounts of every kind of meat, poultry, and fish; unlimited amounts of pure fats and oils; eggs, most cheeses, many vegetables. Like your steak broiled with butter? Go ahead—

enjoy it and still diet. Like your pork chops fried, your celery stuffed with Roquefort cheese? Enjoy them all—and while you're at it, have a martini or a highball!

What can't you eat on a low-carbohydrate diet? In general, try to forget cereals, bread, cakes, and most grain products, including pasta. Also on your not-to-be-eaten-often list: candy, most fresh and all dried fruits, fruit juices, ice cream and sherbet, pastries, sweet beverages, beer, and starchy vegetables, such as corn, potatoes, lima beans, and peas.

If you're an experienced low-calorie dieter, begin now to unlearn some old ideas and habits. For example, a cup of low-fat skim milk contains almost 3 more carbohydrate grams than a cup of whole milk—and over 7 more grams than heavy cream! Which means, on a low-carbohydrate diet, it's better to add heavy cream to your coffee than skim milk! Other examples: carrots are too "expensive" for nibbling (each contains 7 grams), but Cheddar cheese isn't (½ gram per ounce); an old diet standby, chilled fruit-flavored gelatin, contains a whopping 34 grams per cup, but a tablespoon of peanut butter atop a saltine totals just 5 grams. Remember, calories don't necessarily count on a low-carbohydrate diet; therefore, experienced dieters must beware of foods that are low in calories but relatively high in carbohydrate grams.

The magic number on a low-carbohydrate diet is 60. Cut your carbohydrate intake to 60 grams daily and you should lose 10–15 pounds a month. To shed weight more quickly, you can cut your carbohydrate intake still further. But, to play it safe, nutritionists recommend that you consume no fewer than 30 carbohydrate grams a day. Like many diets, a low-carbohydrate diet may seem to lose its effectiveness after two or three weeks. If that is how it works with you—if your weight stays at the same level for a few days, even for a week—don't become discouraged; don't give up. Soon, you'll begin to lose again and (in most cases) at the earlier speedy rate.

Before you start this diet (or **any** diet!), be certain to get your doctor's approval. And after you've begun, use your good sense in choosing the foods you eat. Protect your heart by watching your intake of saturated fats (dieting or not dieting, you should do that!); protect your overall health by including many protein-rich foods (eggs, cheese, fish, meat) and foods rich in vitamins and minerals, or by supplementing your diet with a daily multivitamin. Finally, bear in mind that if you remain on a low-carbohydrate diet for more than two weeks, be sure to include limited—but daily —quantities of milk, citrus fruits and grain products.

Satisfy your sweet tooth on a low-carbohydrate diet by utilizing artificial sweeteners, by sampling sugar-free canned fruits and other desserts, by cultivating a taste for fresh strawberries, cherries, raspberries, and cantaloupe—fruits "cheapest" in carbohydrate content. (When you yearn for a gooey hot fudge sundae, tell yourself that a low-carbohydrate diet not only takes off pounds but helps reduce tooth decay as well. It's true—ask your dentist.) Learn to snack on little chunks of cheese, on bacon bits, sardines, shrimp, chicken livers, and other high-protein foods. You don't ever have to be hungry on a low-carbohydrate diet; the trick is simply in knowing which foods to eat.

ABOUT THIS EDITION

Most of the carbohydrate-gram counts in this new edition of
The Carbohydrate Gram Counter are based on the latest data
published by the United States Department of Agriculture
(handbooks no. 8 and no. 456). Discrepancies between
figures in this edition of The Carbohydrate Gram Counter and
earlier editions are the result of new research and data.

You will note that this edition does not list foods prepared
by home recipe—tuna salad, meat loaf, rice pudding, etc.
The variations in home recipes are so wide it just isn't possi-
ble to calculate carbohydrate grams accurately. Chances
are, your tuna salad is different from your neighbor's tuna
salad, which is also different from the tuna salad served at
a local restaurant. Rather than estimate carbohydrate grams
in homemade foods, it was decided to delete such listings
entirely. However, you can calculate the carbohydrate content
of your tuna salad. Just look up each ingredient you use,
then total the various figures. Divide the total by the number
of servings to find the carbohydrate grams per serving.

Pay attention to portions specified and bear in mind that

measures are level (1 level cup, 1 level teaspoon, etc.) Nobody expects you to use a tape measure to be sure an apple is exactly 2½ inches in diameter, but you can recognize the difference between a small apple and a larger one. If you eat the large one but charge yourself for the small, you're cheating yourself.

Use this book as you would use a dictionary—looking up foods alphabetically. Carry your gram counter wherever you go, refer to it before you plan each of your meals, before you reach for any snack. Remember, until you learn the important gram counts by heart, one "little" error—such as a 52-gram piece of coffee cake—can destroy your entire day!

ABBREVIATIONS USED IN THIS BOOK

fl. oz. ....fluid ounce or fluid ounces
lb. ....pound
oz. ....ounce or ounces
qt. ....quart
tbsp. ....tablespoon or tablespoons
tsp. ....teaspoon or teaspoons
tr. ....trace
″ ....inch or inches

GRAM COUNTS
FROM A TO Z

Listed alphabetically, the carbohydrate
content of over 2,000 foods and drinks.

A

grams

Abalone
    Canned, 4 oz. 2.6
    Raw, in shell, 1 lb. 6.5
    Raw, meat only, 4 oz. 4.2
Acerola
    Fresh, 1 lb. 25.3
    Fresh, 10 fruits 5.6
Acerola juice, fresh, 1 cup 11.6
Albacore (see Tuna)
Alcoholic beverages (see separate listings, pages 130–32)
Alewife, fresh or canned 0
Almond meal, partially defatted, 1 oz. 8.2
Almonds
    Dried, 10 nuts 2.0
    Dried, chopped, 1 cup 25.4
    Dried, chopped, 1 tbsp. 1.6
    Dried, in shell, 1 cup 6.1
    Dried, in shell, 1 lb. 45.1
    Dried, in shell, 4 oz. 8.9

Dried, shelled, 1 cup 27.7
Dried, shelled, 1 lb. 88.5
Dried, shelled, 4 oz. 22.1
Roasted in oil, salted, 1 cup 30.6
Roasted in oil, salted, 1 lb. 88.5
Roasted in oil, salted, 4 oz. 22.1
Slivered, packed, 1 cup 26.3
Sugar- or chocolate-coated (see Candy)
Amaranth leaves, raw, 1 lb. 29.5
Anchovies
   Canned, 2-oz. can 1
   Canned, 5 fillets 1
Apple butter
   1 cup 132.0
   1 tbsp. 8.2
Apple juice
   Canned, 1 cup 29.5
   Canned, 1 fl. oz. 3.7
Apples
   Dehydrated, cooked, sweetened, 1 cup 50.0
   Dehydrated, uncooked, 1 cup 92.1
   Dried, cooked, sweetened, 1 cup 81.8
   Dried, cooked, unsweetened, 1 cup 51.8
   Dried, uncooked, 1 cup 61.0
   Dried, uncooked, 1 lb. 325.7
   Dried, uncooked, 8 oz. 162.9
   Fresh, peeled, 1 apple (3″ diameter) 21.8
   Fresh, peeled, 1 apple (2½″ diameter) 13.9
   Fresh, peeled, quartered, 1 cup 17.6

Fresh, peeled, sliced or diced, 1 cup 15.5
Fresh, with skin, 1 lb. 60.5
Fresh, with skin, 1 apple (3" diameter) 24.0
Fresh, with skin, 1 apple (2½" diameter) 15.3
Fresh, with skin, quartered, 1 cup 18.1
Fresh, with skin, sliced or diced, 1 cup 16.0
Frozen, sweetened, sliced, 8 oz. 55.1

Applesauce
Canned, sweetened, 8 oz. 54.0
Canned, sweetened, 1 cup 60.7
Canned, unsweetened, 8 oz. 24.5
Canned, unsweetened, 1 cup 26.4

Apricot nectar
Canned, 1 cup 36.6
Canned, 1 fl. oz. 4.6

Apricots
Candied, 1 oz. 24.5
Canned, 4 halves with 2 tbsp. heavy syrup 19.8
Canned, halves, heavy syrup, with liquid, 1 cup ...56.8
Canned, halves, water pack, with liquid, 1 cup ...23.6
Dried, 1 cup (about 28 large halves) 86.5
Dried, 8 oz. 150.8
Dried, cooked, sweetened, 1 cup 84.8
Dried, cooked, unsweetened, 1 cup 54.0
Fresh, 1 lb. 54.6
Fresh, 3 apricots (12 per lb.) 13.7
Fresh, pitted, halves, 1 cup 19.8
Frozen, sweetened, 8 oz. 57.0

Artichoke hearts, frozen, 2 hearts 5.0

Artichokes

French or globe, boiled, drained, 4 oz. 10.3

French or globe, raw, 1 lb. 19.2

Jerusalem (see Jerusalem artichokes)

Asparagus

Canned, drained, cut spears, 1 cup 8.0

Canned, drained, whole spears, 4 spears (½″ base) 2.7

Canned, with liquid, 8 oz. 6.6

Fresh, boiled, drained, 4 medium spears (½″ base) 2.2

Fresh, boiled, drained, 4 small spears (⅜″ base). .1.4

Fresh, boiled, drained, cut spears, 1 cup 5.2

Fresh, boiled, drained, whole spears, 1 cup 6.5

Fresh, raw, 1 lb. 22.7

Fresh, raw, cut spears, 1 cup 6.8

Frozen, boiled, drained, cut spears, 1 cup 6.3

Frozen, boiled, drained, whole spears, 4 spears
(½″ base) 2.3

Frozen, boiled, drained, whole spears, 4 spears
(⅜″ base) 1.5

Avocados

California, 1 average avocado (3⅛″ diameter) ...12.9

California, ½ average avocado (3⅛″ diameter) ...6.5

California, cubed, 1 cup 9.0

Florida, 1 average avocado (3⅝″ diameter) 26.7

Florida, ½ average avocado (3⅝″ diameter) 13.5

Florida, cubed, 1 cup 13.2

B

Bacon
    Canadian, fried, drained, 1 lb. 1.4
    Canadian, fried, drained, 1 slice 1
    Fried, drained, 2 medium slices (20 per lb. raw) .. .5
    Fried, drained, 2 thick slices (12 per lb. raw) 8
    Fried, drained, 2 thin slices (28 per lb. raw) 3
Baking powder
    Phosphate, 1 tsp. 1.1
    SAS, 1 tsp. 9
    Tartrate, 1 tsp. 5
Bamboo shoots
    Raw, 1 lb. 23.6
    Raw, cuts, 1 cup 7.9
Bananas
    Fresh, 1 large banana (9¾" long) 30.2
    Fresh, 1 medium banana (8¾" long) 26.4
    Fresh, 1 small banana (7¾" long) 21.1
    Fresh, baking type (plantain), 1 small banana
       (11" long) 82.0

Fresh, mashed, 1 cup 50.0
Fresh, red, 1 average banana (7¼" long) 30.7
Fresh, red, sliced, 1 cup 35.1
Fresh, sliced, 1 cup 33.3
Fresh, with skin, 1 lb. 68.5
Barbecue sauce (see Sauces)
Barley, pearled
Light, uncooked, 1 cup 157.6
Scotch, uncooked, 1 cup 154.4
Bass, fresh or canned 0
Bean curd (tofu)
Soy, 4 oz. 2.7
Soy, 1 cake (2½" × 2¾" × 1") 2.9
Bean sprouts, mung
Boiled, drained, 1 cup 6.5
Raw, 1 cup 6.9
Beans
Baked, canned, with franks and tomato sauce,
1 cup 32.1
Baked, canned, with franks and tomato sauce,
8 oz. 28.6
Baked, canned, with pork and molasses sauce,
1 cup 53.8
Baked, canned, with pork and molasses sauce,
8 oz. 47.9
Baked, canned, with pork and tomato sauce,
1 cup 48.5
Baked, canned, with pork and tomato sauce,
8 oz. 43.1

Baked, canned, with tomato sauce (meatless),
  1 cup 58.7
Baked, canned, with tomato sauce (meatless),
  8 oz. 52.2
Broad (see Broad beans)
Great Northern, cooked, 1 cup 38.2
Green or snap, canned, drained, 1 cup 7.0
Green or snap, canned, with liquid, 1 cup 10.0
Green or snap, fresh, boiled, drained, cut or
  French style, 1 cup 6.8
Green or snap, fresh, raw, cuts, 1 cup 7.8
Green or snap, fresh, raw, cuts, 1 lb. 32.2
Green or snap, frozen, boiled, drained, cuts or
  French style, 1 cup 7.7
Lima, immature seeds, baby, frozen, boiled,
  drained, 1 cup 40.1
Lima, immature seeds, boiled, drained, 1 cup 33.7
Lima, immature seeds, canned, drained, 1 cup 31.1
Lima, immature seeds, canned, with liquid, 1 cup..33.2
Lima, immature seeds, Fordhook, frozen, boiled,
  drained, 1 cup 32.5
Lima, immature seeds, raw, 1 cup 34.3
Lima, immature seeds, raw, 1 lb. 100.2
Pea, navy, or white, cooked, 1 cup 40.3
Pinto, mature seeds, dried, 1 cup 121.0
Red kidney, canned, with liquid, 1 cup 41.8
Red kidney, cooked, 1 cup 39.6
Red kidney, raw, 1 cup 114.5
Wax or yellow, boiled, drained, cuts, 1 cup 5.8

Wax or yellow, canned, drained, 1 cup 7.0
Wax or yellow, canned, with liquid, 1 cup 10.0
Wax or yellow, frozen, boiled, drained, cuts,
   1 cup 8.4
Wax or yellow, raw, cuts, 1 cup 6.6
Wax or yellow, raw, cuts, 1 lb. 27.2

Beechnuts
In shell, 1 lb. 56.2
In shell, 4 oz. 14.1
Shelled, 1 lb. 92.1
Shelled, 4 oz. 23.0

Beef
Boiled, braised, or pot-roasted 0
Brains (see Brains)
Brisket 0
Chuck 0
Corned 0
Corned, hash (see Hash)
Dried, chipped 0
Dried, chipped, creamed, 1 cup 17.4
Flank 0
Ground 0
Hamburger 0
Heart (see Heart)
Kidney (see Kidney)
Liver (see Liver)
Loin 0
Plate 0
Potted 0

Rib 0
Roast 0
Round 0
Rump 0
Short ribs 0
Steak 0
Stewing 0
Tongue (see Tongue)
Beef pot pie, frozen, 8-oz. pie 40.8
Beef-vegetable stew
    Canned, 1 cup 17.4
    Canned, 8 oz. 16.1
Beer (see Alcoholic Beverages, pages 130-32)
Beet greens
    Boiled, drained, 1 cup 4.8
    Raw, trimmed, 1 lb. 11.7
Beets
    Boiled, drained, 2 whole beets (2" diameter) 7.2
    Boiled, drained, diced or sliced, 1 cup 12.2
    Canned, drained, diced or sliced, 1 cup 15.0
    Canned, drained, whole small, 1 cup 14.1
    Canned, with liquid, 1 cup 19.4
    Raw, peeled, 1 lb. 44.9
    Raw, peeled, diced or sliced, 1 cup 13.4
Beverages (see individual listings)
Biscuit, mix, made with milk, 1-oz. biscuit 14.6
Blackberry juice, canned, unsweetened, 1 cup 19.1
Blackberries
    Canned, heavy syrup, with liquid, 1 cup 56.8

Canned, heavy syrup, with liquid, 1 lb. 100.7
Canned, water pack, with liquid, 1 cup 22.0
Canned, water pack, with liquid, 1 lb. 40.8
Fresh, 1 cup 18.6
Fresh, 1 lb. 55.6
Frozen, sweetened, 1 cup 34.9
Frozen, sweetened, 1 lb. 110.7
Frozen, unsweetened, 1 cup 14.4
Frozen, unsweetened, 1 lb. 51.7

Blood pudding or sausage
1 lb. 1.4
4 oz. 4

Blueberries
Fresh, 1 cup 22.2
Fresh, 1 lb. 63.8
Frozen, sweetened, 1 cup 61.0
Frozen, sweetened, 1 lb. 120.2
Frozen, unsweetened, 1 cup 22.4
Frozen, unsweetened, 1 lb. 61.7

Bluefish 0

Bockwurst
1 lb. (approx. 7 links) 2.7
4 oz. 7
1 link 4

Bologna
All meat, 1 lb. 16.8
All meat, 4 oz. 4.2
With cereal, 1 lb. 17.7

With cereal, 4 oz. 4.5
Bouillon
    Cube, 1 cube (½") 2
    Instant powder, 1 tsp. 1
Boysenberries
    Canned, water pack, with liquid, 1 cup 22.2
    Canned, water pack, with liquid, 1 lb. 41.3
    Frozen, sweetened, 1 cup 34.9
    Frozen, sweetened, 1 lb. 110.7
    Fresh, 1 lb. 55.6
    Frozen, unsweetened, 1 cup 14.4
    Frozen, unsweetened, 1 lb. 51.7
Brains, all kinds, raw, 4 oz. 9
Bran or bran flakes (see Cereals, Wheat bran)
Braunschweiger
    1 lb. 10.4
    4 oz. 2.6
Brazil nuts
    3 large nuts 1.5
    In shell, 1 cup 6.4
    In shell, 1 lb. 23.7
    In shell, 4 oz. 5.9
    Shelled, 1 cup 15.3
    Shelled, 1 lb. 49.4
    Shelled, 4 oz. 12.4
Bread, commercial
    Boston brown, canned, 1-lb. can 206.8
    Boston brown, canned, 1 slice (3¼" diameter,
        ½" thick) 20.5

Cracked wheat, 1-lb. loaf 236.3
Cracked wheat, 1 slice (20 per loaf) 11.8
French, 1-lb. loaf 251.3
French, 1 slice (2½" × 2" × ½") 8.3
Italian, 1-lb. loaf 255.8
Italian, 1 slice (3¼" × 2½" × ½") 5.6
Pumpernickel, 1-lb. loaf 240.9
Pumpernickel, 1 slice (5" × 4" × ⅜") 17.0
Pumpernickel, 1 party slice (2½" × 2" × ¼")..3.7
Raisin, 1-lb. loaf 243.1
Raisin, 1 slice (20 per loaf)..................12.2
Rye, light, 1-lb. loaf 236.3
Rye, light, 1 slice (20 per loaf) 11.8
Rye, light, 1 party slice (2½" × 2" × ¼") 3.6
Vienna, 1-lb. loaf 251.3
Vienna, 1 slice (4¾" × 4" × ½") 13.9
White, firm-crumb type, 1-lb. loaf 227.7
White, firm-crumb type, 1 slice (20 per loaf) 11.5
White, soft-crumb type, 1-lb. loaf 229.1
White, soft-crumb type, 1 slice (18 per loaf) 12.6
White, 1 thin slice (26 per loaf) 8.8
Whole wheat, firm-crumb type, 1-lb. loaf 216.4
Whole wheat, firm-crumb type, 1 slice (20 per loaf) 11.0
Whole wheat, soft-crumb type, 1-lb. loaf 223.6
Whole wheat, soft-crumb type, 1 slice (16 per loaf) 13.8
Bread crumbs
    Dried, grated, 1 cup 73.4
    Dried, grated, 1 tbsp. 4.6

Soft, 1 cup 22.7
Bread cubes, soft, 1 cup 15.2
Bread sticks
 Regular, 4 oz. 85.4
 Regular, 1 stick (4½″ long) 7.5
 Vienna type, 4 oz. 65.8
 Vienna type, 1 stick (6½″ long) 20.3
Bread stuffing mix
 Cubes or crumbs, dried, 1 cup 21.7
 Cubes or crumbs, dried, 4 oz. 82.2
 Prepared, crumbly, 1 cup 49.8
 Prepared, moist, 1 cup 39.4
Breadfruit
 Fresh, 1 lb. 91.5
 Fresh, peeled, 4 oz. 29.9
Breakfast cereal (see Cereal)
Broad beans
 Raw, immature seeds, 1 lb. 80.7
 Raw, immature seeds, 4 oz. 20.2
 Raw, mature seeds, 1 lb. 264.0
 Raw, mature seeds, 4 oz. 66.0
Broccoli
 Boiled, drained, 1 lb. 20.4
 Boiled, drained, 1 large stalk 12.6
 Boiled, drained, 1 medium stalk 8.1
 Boiled, drained, 1 small stalk 6.3
 Boiled, drained, cut stalks, 1 cup 7.0
 Frozen, boiled, drained, 1 stalk (4½″ long) 1.4

Frozen, chopped, boiled, drained, 1 cup 8.5
Raw, 1 lb. 16.3
Brussels sprouts
   Boiled, drained, 1 cup 9.9
   Boiled, drained, 1 lb. 29.0
   Boiled, drained, 4 sprouts 5.4
   Frozen, boiled, drained, 1 cup 10.1
   Raw, 1 lb. 37.6
Buckwheat flour (see Flour)
Bulgur (parboiled wheat)
   Canned, seasoned, 1 cup 44.3
   Canned, unseasoned, 1 cup 47.3
   Dried, club wheat, 1 cup 139.1
   Dried, hard red winter wheat, 1 cup 128.7
   Dried, white wheat, 1 cup 121.1
Burbot 0
Butter, salted or unsalted
   Regular, 1 cup 9
   Regular, 1 stick (1/4" lb.) 5
   Regular, 1 tbsp. 1
   Regular, 1 pat ....tr.
   Regular or whipped, 1 lb. 1.8
   Whipped, 1 cup 6
   Whipped, 1 tbsp. ....tr.
   Whipped, 1 pat ....tr.
Butterfish 0
Buttermilk (see Milk)
Butternuts
   In shell, 1 lb. 5.3

In shell, 4 oz. 1.3
Shelled, 1 lb. 38.1
Shelled, 4 oz. 9.5

C

grams

Cabbage

    Chinese, raw, 1 lb. 13.2

    Chinese, raw, 1″ pieces, 1 cup 2.3

    Red, raw, 1 lb. 28.2

    Red, raw, chopped or fine shredded, 1 cup 6.2

    Red, raw, sliced or coarse shredded, 1 cup 4.8

    Savoy, raw, 1 lb. 18.8

    Savoy, raw, coarse shredded, 1 cup 3.2

    Spoon, boiled, drained, cuts, 1 cup 4.1

    Spoon, raw, 1 lb. 13.2

    Spoon, raw, 1″ pieces, 1 cup 2.0

    White, boiled, drained, shredded, 1 cup 6.2

    White, boiled, drained, wedges, 1 cup 6.8

    White, raw, 1 lb. 22.0

    White, raw, chopped or fine shredded, 1 cup 4.9

    White, raw, sliced or coarse shredded, 1 cup 3.8

Cabbage salad (see Coleslaw)

Cake

    Frozen, devil's food, chocolate icing, 1 cake

(7½" diameter) 283.6

Frozen, devil's food, chocolate icing,
3½-oz. serving 55.6

Cake icing (see Icing)

Cake mix, prepared as directed on package

Angel food, without icing, 1 cake (9¾" diameter) 377.2

Angel food, without icing, 3½-oz. serving 59.4

Chocolate malt, white icing, 1 cake (9" diameter) 710.0

Chocolate malt, white icing, 3½-oz. serving 66.6

Coffee cake, without icing, 1 cake (7¾" diameter) 225.3

Coffee cake, without icing, 3½-oz. serving 52.4

Cupcake, without icing, 1 cake (2¾" diameter) ..18.4

Cupcake, chocolate icing, 1 cake (2¾" diameter) 28.4

Devil's food, chocolate icing, 1 cake (8" diameter) 645.4

Devil's food, chocolate icing, 3½-oz. serving 58.3

Gingerbread, without icing, 1 cake (8¼"
diameter) 291.3

Gingerbread, without icing, 3½-oz. serving 51.1

Honey-spice, caramel icing, 1 cake (8" diameter) 752.1

Honey-spice, caramel icing, 3½-oz. serving 60.9

Marble, white icing, 1 cake (8" diameter) 647.9

Marble, white icing, 3½-oz. serving 62.0

White, chocolate icing, 1 cake (9" diameter) ...715.9

White, chocolate icing, 3½-oz. serving 62.8

Yellow, chocolate icing, 1 cake (8" diameter) ...638.2

Yellow, chocolate icing, 3½-oz. serving 57.6

Candied fruit (see individual listings)

Candy

Almonds, chocolate-coated, 1 cup 65.3

Almonds, chocolate-coated, 1 oz. 11.2
Almonds, sugar-coated, 1 cup 136.9
Almonds, sugar-coated, 1 oz. 19.9
Butterscotch, 1 oz. 26.9
Candy corn, 1 cup 179.2
Candy corn, 1 oz. 25.4
Caramel, chocolate or vanilla, 1 oz. 21.7
Chocolate, bittersweet, 1 oz. 13.3
Chocolate, milk, plain, 1 oz. 16.1
Chocolate, milk, with almonds, 1 oz. 14.5
Chocolate, milk, with peanuts, 1 oz. 12.6
Chocolate, semisweet, 1 oz. 16.2
Chocolate, sweet, 1 oz. 16.4
Chocolate disks, sugar-coated, 1 cup 143.2
Chocolate disks, sugar-coated, 1 oz. 20.6
Chocolate-flavored roll, 1 oz. 23.4
Coconut, chocolate-coated, 1 oz. 20.4
Fondant, chocolate-coated, 1 oz. 23.0
Fondant, plain, 1 oz. 25.4
Fudge, chocolate or vanilla, 1 oz. 21.3
Fudge, with caramel and peanuts, chocolate-coated,
   1 oz. 18.2
Fudge, with nuts, 1 oz. 19.6
Gumdrops, 1 oz. 24.8
Hard candy, 1 oz. 27.6
Honeycomb with peanut butter, chocolate-coated,
   1 oz. 20.0
Jelly beans, 1 cup 204.8
Jelly beans, 1 oz. 26.4

Marshmallow, 1 oz. 22.8
Marshmallow, 1 large (1⅛″ diameter) 5.8
Marshmallow, miniature, 1 cup 37.0
Mints, chocolate-coated, 1 oz. 23.0
Mints, chocolate-coated, 1 large (2½″ diameter)..28.4
Mints, uncoated, 1 oz. 25.4
Mints, uncoated, 1 large (1½″ diameter) 7.9
Peanut bar, 1 oz. 13.4
Peanut brittle, 1 oz. 23.0
Peanuts, chocolate-coated, 1 cup 66.5
Peanuts, chocolate-coated, 1 oz. 11.1
Raisins, chocolate-coated, 1 cup 134.0
Raisins, chocolate-coated, 1 oz. 20.0
Vanilla creams, chocolate-coated, 1 oz. 19.9

Cantaloupe
Fresh, 1 lb. 17.0
Fresh, 1 melon (5″ diameter) 39.8
Fresh, ½ melon (5″ diameter) 20.4
Fresh, diced, 1 cup 12.0

Capicola 0
Carp 0

Carrots
Boiled, drained, diced, 1 cup 10.3
Boiled, drained, sliced, 1 cup 11.0
Canned, drained, diced, 1 cup 9.7
Canned, drained, sliced, 1 cup 10.4
Canned, with liquid, 1 cup 16.0
Dehydrated, 1 oz. 23.0
Raw, 1 carrot (7½″ long) 7.0

Raw, 6–8 strips (¼" × 2½") 2.7
Raw, grated or shredded, 1 cup 10.7
Raw, whole, without tops, 1 lb. 44.0

Casaba melon
Fresh, diced, 1 cup 11.1
Fresh, whole with rind, 1 lb. 14.7
Fresh, 1 wedge (2" × 7¾") 9.1

Cashew nuts
Roasted in oil, 1 lb. 132.9
Roasted in oil, 4 oz. 33.3
Roasted in oil, whole, 1 cup 41.0

Catsup
Tomato, bottled, 1 cup 69.3
Tomato, bottled, 1 tbsp. 3.8

Cauliflower
Boiled, drained, flower buds, 1 cup 5.1
Boiled, drained, flower buds, 1 lb. 18.6
Frozen, boiled, drained, 1 cup 5.9
Frozen, boiled, drained, 1 lb. 15.0
Raw, flower buds only, 1 lb. 23.6
Raw, flower buds only, chopped, 1 cup 6.0
Raw, flower buds only, sliced, 1 cup 4.4

Caviar, sturgeon
Granular, 1 oz. 9
Granular, 1 tbsp. 5
Pressed, 1 oz. 1.4
Pressed, 1 tbsp. 8

Celeriac root, raw, pared, 4 oz. 9.7

Celery

Boiled, drained, chopped or diced, 1 cup 4.7
Raw, 1 lb. 15.8
Raw, 1 outer stalk (8″ long) 1.6
Raw, 3 inner stalks (5″ long) 2.0
Raw, chopped or diced, 1 oz. 1.1
Raw, chopped or diced, 1 cup 4.7

Celery cabbage (see Cabbage, Chinese)

Cereal

Bran, with sugar and defatted wheat germ, 1 cup..59.1
Bran, with sugar and malt extract, 1 cup 44.6
Bran flakes, 40%, 1 cup 28.2
Bran flakes with raisins, 1 cup 39.7
Corn, puffed, 1 cup 16.2
Corn, puffed, presweetened, 1 cup 26.9
Corn, puffed, presweetened, cocoa-flavored, 1 cup..26.0
Corn, puffed, presweetened, fruit-flavored, 1 cup..26.2
Corn, shredded, 1 cup 21.7
Corn flakes, 1 cup 21.3
Corn flakes, sugar-coated, 1 cup 36.5
Farina, instant, cooked, 1 cup 27.9
Farina, quick, cooked, 1 cup 21.8
Farina, regular, cooked, 1 cup 21.3
Oat flakes, maple-flavored, cooked, 1 cup 31.2
Oat granules, maple-flavored, cooked, 1 cup 27.9
Oatmeal or rolled oats, cooked, 1 cup 23.3
Oats, puffed, 1 cup 18.8
Oats, shredded, 1 cup 32.4
Oats and corn, puffed, sugar-coated, 1 cup 30.0

Oats and wheat, cooked, 1 cup 29.6
Rice, granulated, cooked, 1 cup 27.4
Rice, oven-popped, 1 cup 26.3
Rice, oven-popped, presweetened, 1 cup 40.8
Rice, puffed, 1 cup 13.4
Rice, puffed, with honey or cocoa, 1 cup 30.3
Rice, shredded, 1 cup 22.2
Wheat, puffed, 1 cup 11.8
Wheat, puffed, with sugar, 1 cup 30.9
Wheat, rolled, cooked, 1 cup 40.6
Wheat, shredded, 1 oblong biscuit
  (2½" × 2" × 1¼") 20.0
Wheat, shredded, 1 round biscuit (3" diameter) ..16.0
Wheat, shredded, crumbled, 1 cup 28.0
Wheat, shredded, spoon size, 1 cup 40.0
Wheat, whole-meal, cooked, 1 cup 23.0
Wheat and malted barley, toasted, instant-cooked,
  1 cup 39.4
Wheat and malted barley, toasted, quick-cooked,
  1 cup 32.3
Wheat and malted barley flakes, 1 cup 33.7
Wheat and malted barley granules, 1 cup 92.8
Wheat flakes, 1 cup 24.2
Wheat germ, 1 tbsp. 3.0
Cervelat
Dried, 1 lb. 7.7
Dried, 4 oz. 1.9
Soft, 1 lb. 7.3
Soft, 4 oz. 1.8

Chard
Swiss, boiled, drained, leaves, 1 cup 5.8
Swiss, boiled, drained, leaves and stems, 1 cup ...4.8
Swiss, raw, whole, 1 lb. 20.9
Cheese
American, processed, 1 cubic inch 3
American, processed, 1 oz. 5
American, processed, diced, 1 cup 2.7
American, processed, shredded, 1 cup 2.1
American, processed, shredded, 1 tbsp. 1
Blue or Roquefort, 1 cubic inch 3
Blue or Roquefort, 1 oz. 6
Blue or Roquefort, crumbled, 1 cup 2.7
Blue or Roquefort, crumbled, 1 cup packed 5.0
Brick, 1 cubic inch 3
Brick, 1 oz. 5
Camembert, domestic, 1 cubic inch 3
Camembert, domestic, 1 cup 4.4
Camembert, domestic, 1 oz. 5
Cheddar, domestic, 1 cubic inch 4
Cheddar, domestic, 1 lb. 9.5
Cheddar, domestic, 1 oz. 6
Cheddar, domestic, shredded, 1 cup 2.4
Cheddar, domestic, shredded, 1 tbsp. 1
Cottage, creamed, 1 oz. 8
Cottage, creamed, large curd, 1 cup 6.5
Cottage, creamed, large or small curd, 1 cup packed 7.1
Cottage, creamed, small curd, 1 cup 6.1
Cottage, uncreamed, 1 cup 3.9

Cottage, uncreamed, 1 cup packed 5.4
Cottage, uncreamed, 1 oz. 8
Cream, 1 cubic inch 3
Cream, 1 cup 4.9
Cream, 1 tbsp. 3
Cream, 1 oz. 6
Cream, whipped, 1 cup 3.3
Cream, whipped, 1 tbsp. 2
Cream, whipped, 1 oz. 6
Limburger, 1 cubic inch 4
Limburger, 1 oz. 6
Parmesan, 1 oz. 8
Parmesan, grated, 1 cup 3.5
Parmesan, grated, 1 cup packed 4.9
Parmesan, grated, 1 tbsp. 2
Parmesan, shredded, 1 cup 2.4
Parmesan, shredded, 1 cup packed 3.3
Parmesan, shredded, 1 tbsp. 2
Pimiento, processed, 1 cubic inch 3
Pimiento, processed, 1 oz. 5
Swiss, domestic, 1 cubic inch 3
Swiss, domestic, 1 lb. 7.7
Swiss, domestic, 1 oz. 5
Cheese food
    American, processed, 1 oz. 2.0
    American, processed, 1 tbsp. 1.0
Cheese spread
    American, 1 oz. 2.3
    American, 1 tbsp. 1.1

Cheese straws

    1 oz. 9.8

    10 pieces (5" long) 20.7

Cherimoya, raw, 1 fruit (5" diameter) 117.2

Cherries

    Candied, 1 oz. 24.6

    Candied, 1 average cherry 3.0

    Maraschino, bottled, with liquid, 1 oz. 8.3

    Sour red, canned, pitted, water pack, with liquid,

      1 cup 26.1

    Sour red, fresh, pitted, 1 cup 22.2

    Sour red, fresh, pitted, 1 lb. 64.9

    Sour red, fresh, whole, 1 cup 14.7

    Sour red, fresh, whole, 1 lb. 52.5

    Sour red, frozen, sweetened, 1 lb. 126.1

    Sour red, frozen, sweetened, 4 oz. 31.5

    Sour red, frozen, unsweetened, 1 lb. 60.8

    Sour red, frozen, unsweetened, 4 oz. 15.2

    Sweet, canned pitted, heavy syrup, with liquid,

      1 cup 52.7

    Sweet, canned, whole, heavy syrup, with liquid,

      1 cup 52.6

    Sweet, canned, water pack, with liquid, 1 cup 29.6

    Sweet, fresh, 10 cherries 11.7

    Sweet, fresh, pitted, 1 cup 25.2

    Sweet, fresh, pitted, 1 lb. 78.9

    Sweet, fresh, whole, 1 cup 20.4

    Sweet, fresh, whole, 1 lb. 71.0

Chervil, raw, 1 oz. 3.3

Chestnuts

    Dried, in shell, 4 oz. 73.1

    Dried, shelled, 4 oz. 89.1

    Fresh, 10 nuts 30.7

    Fresh, in shell, 1 cup 40.9

    Fresh, in shell, 1 lb. 154.7

    Fresh, in shell, 4 oz. 38.7

    Fresh, shelled, 1 cup 67.4

    Fresh, shelled, 1 lb. 191.0

    Fresh, shelled, 4 oz. 47.8

Chewing gum (see Gum)

Chicken

    Boiled, roasted, or stewed back 0

    Boiled, roasted, or stewed breast 0

    Boiled, roasted, or stewed drumstick 0

    Boiled, roasted, or stewed neck 0

    Boiled, roasted, or stewed rib section 0

    Boiled, roasted, or stewed thigh 0

    Boiled, roasted, or stewed wing 0

    Canned or potted 0

Chicken chow mein (see Chow mein)

Chicken gizzards

    Raw, 4 oz. 8

    Simmered, chopped or diced, 1 cup 1.0

Chicken heart (see Heart)

Chicken liver (see Liver)

Chicken pot pie, frozen, 8-oz. pie 50.4

Chickpeas

    Dry, 4 oz. 69.5

Dry, 1 cup 122.0
Chicory, Witloof (see Endive, French or Belgian)
Chicory greens, raw, untrimmed, 1 lb. 14.1
Chili con carne
    With beans, canned, 1 cup 31.1
    With beans, canned, 1 lb. 55.3
Chili powder, with added seasonings, 1 tbsp. 3.3
Chili sauce
    Tomato, bottled, 1 cup 67.7
    Tomato, bottled, 1 tbsp. 3.7
Chives
    Fresh, whole, 1 lb. 26.3
    Fresh, chopped, 1 tbsp. 2
    Fresh, chopped, 1 tsp. 1
Chocolate
    Bitter or baking, unsweetened, 1 oz. 8.2
    Bitter or baking, unsweetened, grated, 1 cup 38.1
    Semisweet chips or morsels, 1 cup 96.9
Chocolate candy (see Candy)
Chocolate milk (see Milk)
Chocolate syrup (see Syrup)
Chop suey
    With meat, without noodles, 1 cup 12.8
    With meat, without noodles, 1 lb. 23.1
Chow mein
    Chicken, canned, without noodles, 1 cup. 17.8
    Chicken, canned, without noodles, 1 lb. 18.1
Chub 0
Cider (see Apple juice)

Citron, candied, 1 oz. 22.7
Clam chowder (see Soup)
Clam juice, canned, 1 cup 5.0
Clams
    Canned, drained, 4 oz. 2.2
    Canned, drained, diced or minced, 1 cup 3.0
    Canned, with liquid, 4 oz. 3.2
    Hard or round, raw, meat only, 4 oz. 6.7
    Hard or round, raw, meat only, 5 clams 4.1
    Soft, raw, meat only, 4 oz. 1.5
Cocoa
    Beverage powder, dry, 1 oz. (4 heaping tsp.) 25.3
    Dry powder, high, medium fat, 1 tbsp. 2.8
    Dry powder, high, medium fat, with alkali, 1 tbsp...2.6
    Dry powder, low, medium fat, 1 tbsp. 2.9
    Dry powder low, medium fat, with alkali, 1 tbsp....2.7
Coconut
    Dried, sweetened, 4 oz. 60.3
    Dried, unsweetened, 4 oz. 26.1
    Fresh, shredded, 1 cup 7.5
    Fresh, shredded or grated, 1 cup packed 12.2
    Fresh, 1 coconut (4⅝" diameter) 37.3
    Fresh, 1 piece (2" × 2" × 2") 4.2
Coconut cream
    From grated coconut meat, 1 cup 19.9
    From grated coconut meat, 1 tbsp. 1.2
Coconut milk (grated coconut meat and water), 1 cup..12.5
Coconut water, liquid from coconut, 1 cup 11.3
Cod, fresh, canned, dried or broiled 0

Cod cakes (see Fish cakes)
Coffee, prepared, plain, 1 gallon ....tr.
Cola (see Soft drinks)
Coleslaw, commercial
    With French dressing, 1 cup 9.1
    With mayonnaise, 1 cup 5.8
    With salad dressing (mayonnaise type), 1 cup 8.5
Collards
    Boiled in large amount water, drained, leaves,
       1 cup 9.1
    Boiled in small amount water, drained, leaves,
       1 cup 9.7
    Frozen, boiled, drained, chopped, 1 cup 9.5
    Raw, with stems, 1 lb. 32.7
Cookies, commercial
    Animal crackers, 1 oz. 22.6
    Animal crackers, 1 average piece 2.1
    Assorted, 1 lb. (52 cookies) 322.1
    Assorted, 1 oz. 20.1
    Brownies with nuts, iced, frozen, 1
       ($1\frac{1}{2}'' \times 1\frac{3}{4}'' \times \frac{7}{8}''$) 14.9
    Butter thins, 1 lb. (90 cookies) 321.6
    Butter thins, 1 oz. 20.1
    Butter thins, 1 piece (2" diameter) 5.5
    Chocolate, 1 oz. 20.3
    Chocolate chip, 1 lb. (43 cookies) 316.2
    Chocolate chip, 1 oz. 19.8
    Chocolate chip, 1 piece ($2\frac{1}{4}''$ diameter) 7.3
    Coconut bars, 1 oz. 18.1

Coconut bars, 10 cookies (2⅜" × 1⅝" × ⅜")..57.5
Cream sandwiches, 1 oz. 19.6
Cream sandwiches, oval, 1 piece 10.4
Cream sandwich, round, 1 piece (1¾" diameter)...6.9
Fig bars, 1 lb. (32 cookies) 342.0
Fig bars, 1 oz. 21.4
Fig bars, 1 average piece 10.6
Gingersnaps, 1 lb. (65 cookies) 362.0
Gingersnaps, 1 oz. 22.6
Gingersnaps, 1 piece (2" diameter) 5.6
Graham crackers, chocolate-coated, 1 oz. 19.3
Graham crackers, chocolate-coated, 1 piece
   (2½" × 2") 8.8
Graham crackers, plain, 1 oz. 20.8
Graham crackers, plain, 1 piece (5" × 2½") 10.4
Graham crackers, sugar-honey, 1 oz. 21.7
Graham crackers, sugar-honey, 1 piece
   (5½" × 2½") 10.8
Ladyfingers, 1 oz. 18.3
Ladyfingers, 1 piece 7.1
Macaroons, 1 lb. (24 cookies) 299.8
Macaroons, 1 oz. 18.7
Macaroons, 1 piece (2¾" diameter) 12.5
Marshmallow, coconut or chocolate-coated, 1 oz...20.5
Marshmallow, coconut or chocolate-coated,
   1 piece (2⅛" diameter) 13.0
Molasses, 1 lb. (14 cookies) 344.7
Molasses, 1 oz. 21.5
Molasses, 1 piece (3⅝" diameter) 24.7

Oatmeal with raisins, 1 lb. 333.4

Oatmeal with raisins, 1 oz. 20.8

Oatmeal with raisins, 1 piece (2⅝" diameter) 9.6

Peanut sandwiches, 1 piece (1¾" diameter) 8.2

Peanut sandwiches or sugar wafers, 1 lb........303.9

Peanut sandwiches or sugar wafers, 1 oz. 19.0

Peanut sugar wafers, 1 average piece 4.7

Raisin, biscuit type, 1 oz. 22.9

Raisin, biscuit type, 1 piece (2¼" × 2" × 1¼") 11.5

Shortbread, 1 lb. (60 cookies) 295.3

Shortbread, 1 oz. 18.5

Shortbread, 1 average piece 4.9

Sugar wafers, 1 oz. 20.8

Sugar wafers, 1 piece (3½" × 1" × ½") 7.0

Vanilla wafers, 1 oz. 21.1

Vanilla wafers, 1 piece (1¾" diameter) 3.0

Vanilla wafers, brown edge, 1 piece (2¾" diameter) 4.3

Cooking oil (see Oil)

Corn

Boiled, drained, kernels, 1 cup 31.0

Boiled, drained, on cob, 1 lb. 52.4

Boiled, drained, on cob, 1 ear (5" × 1¾") 16.2

Canned, cream style, 1 cup 51.2

Canned, kernels, drained, 1 cup 32.7

Canned, vacuum packed, 1 cup 43.1

Frozen, boiled, drained, kernels, 1 cup 31.0

Frozen, boiled, drained, on cob, 1 ear (5" long) ..27.2

Corn flour (see Cornmeal)

Corn grits

Dried, 1 cup 125.0

Cooked, 1 cup 27.0

Corn bread, mix, made with egg and milk, 1 piece
(2½" square) 27.5

Cornmeal

Degermed, cooked, 1 cup 25.7

Degermed, dried, 1 cup 108.2

Whole ground, unbolted, dried, 1 cup 89.9

Cornstarch, 1 cup lightly filled 112.1

Cornstarch, 1 tbsp. 7.0

Cottonseed oil (see Oil)

Cowpeas

Immature seeds (including black-eyed peas),
boiled, drained, 1 cup 29.9

Immature seeds (including black-eyed peas),
canned, with liquid, 1 cup 31.6

Immature seeds (including black-eyed peas),
frozen, boiled, drained, 1 cup 40.0

Immature seeds (including black-eyed peas),
raw, 1 cup 31.6

Mature seeds, cooked, 1 cup 34.5

Mature seeds, dried, 1 cup 104.9

Young pods, with seeds, boiled, drained, 1 cup ...31.8

Crab

Canned, claw, 1 cup 1.3

Canned, drained, 4 oz. 1.3

Canned, white or king, 1 cup 1.5

Canned, white or king, 1 lb. 5.0

Canned, white or king, claw, 1 cup packed 1.8
Fresh, steamed, 1 lb. 2.3
Fresh, steamed, flaked, 1 cup 6
Fresh, steamed, flaked or pieces, 1 cup packed 1.1
Fresh, steamed, meat only, 4 oz. 6
Fresh, steamed, pieces, 1 cup 8
Crab apples, fresh, whole, 1 lb. 74.3
Cracker crumbs
    Butter crackers, 1 cup 53.8
    Graham crackers, 1 cup 62.3
    Graham crackers, 1 cup packed 77.0
    Soda crackers, 1 cup 49.4
Crackers
    Animal (see Cookies)
    Butter, 1 oz. 19.1
    Butter, round, 1 piece (1⅞" diameter) 2.2
    Cheese, 1 oz. 17.1
    Cheese, rectangular sticks, 10 pieces
      (1⅝" diameter) 5.5
    Cheese, round, 1 piece (1⅞" diameter) 2.1
    Graham (see Cookies)
    Oyster or soup, 1 oz. 20.0
    Oyster or soup, 1 cup 31.8
    Oyster or soup, 10 pieces 5.3
    Rusk, 1 oz. 20.1
    Rusk, 1 piece (3⅜" × ½") 6.4
    Rye wafers, 1 lb. 346.1
    Rye wafers, 1 oz. 21.6
    Rye wafers, 1 piece (3½" × 1⅞" × ¼") 5.0

Saltines, 1 oz. 20.3
Saltines, 1 piece (1⅞″ square) 2.0
Sandwich, cheese–peanut butter, 1 oz. 15.9
Sandwich, cheese–peanut butter, 1 piece
   (1⅝″ diameter) 4.0
Soda, 1 oz. 20.0
Soda, 1 piece (1⅞″ square) 2.0
Whole wheat, 1 oz. 19.3
Zwieback, 1 oz. 21.1
Zwieback, 1 piece (3½″ × 1½″ × ½″) 5.2
Cranberries
   Fresh, chopped, 1 cup 11.9
   Fresh, whole, 1 cup 10.3
   Fresh, whole, with stems, 1 lb. 47.0
Cranberry juice cocktail, canned, 1 cup 41.7
Cranberry relish with orange, uncooked, 1 cup 124.9
Cranberry sauce, canned, strained, 1 cup 103.9
Cream
   Half and half, 1 cup 11.1
   Half and half, 1 tbsp. 7
   Light or table, 1 cup 10.3
   Light or table, 1 tbsp. 6
   Sour, 1 cup 9.9
   Sour, 1 tbsp. 5
   Whipping, light, unwhipped, 1 cup 8.6
   Whipping, light, unwhipped, 1 tbsp. 5
   Whipping, light, whipped, 1 cup 4.3
   Whipping, heavy, unwhipped, 1 cup 7.4
   Whipping, heavy, unwhipped, 1 tbsp. 5

Whipping, heavy, whipped, 1 cup 3.7
Cream substitute, nondairy, powder, 1 tbsp. 3.0
Cress
    Garden, boiled in large amount water, drained,
      1 cup 4.9
    Garden, boiled in small amount water, drained,
      1 cup 5.1
    Garden, raw, 1 lb. 17.7
    Water (see Watercress)
Croaker 0
Cucumber
    Peeled, 1 large (8¼″ long) 9.0
    Peeled, 1 small (6⅜″ long) 5.1
    Peeled, 6–7 large slices 9
    Peeled, sliced or diced, 1 cup 4.6
    With skin, 1 lb. 14.7
    With skin, 1 large (8¼″ long) 10.2
    With skin, 1 small (6⅜″ long) 5.8
    With skin, sliced, 1 cup 3.6
Cucumber pickles (see Pickles)
Currants
    Black, fresh, 4 oz. 14.9
    Red or white, fresh, 4 oz. 13.8
Cusk 0

D

Dandelion greens
    Boiled, drained, 1 cup 6.7
    Raw, 1 lb. 41.7
Danish pastry, commercial, plain, 1 piece
    (4½″ diameter) 29.6
Dates, moisturized or hydrated
    Chopped, 1 cup 129.8
    Whole, pitted, 1 lb. 330.7
    Whole, pitted, 4 oz. 82.8
    Whole, pitted, 10 dates 58.3
    Whole, with pits, 1 lb. 287.7
    Whole, with pits, 4 oz. 71.9
    Whole, with pits, 10 dates 58.3
Dewberries, fresh, 1 cup 18.6
Dock or sorrel, raw, trimmed, 4 oz. 6.4
Doughnuts, plain
    Cake type, 1 piece (3⅝″ diameter; 2 oz.) 29.8
    Cake type, 1 piece (3¼″ diameter; 1½ oz.) 21.6

Cake type, 1 piece (1½" diameter; ½ oz.) 7.2
Yeast leavened, 1 piece (3¾" diameter; 1½ oz.)..16.0
Drum, freshwater or red 0
Duck, domesticated or wild 0

E

grams

Eclair, custard-filled, chocolate icing, 1 piece (3½ oz.). 23.2

Eel, fresh or smoked 0

Eggplant

    Boiled, drained, diced, 1 cup 8.2

    Raw, whole, 1 lb. 20.6

Eggs

    Chicken, boiled, poached, or scrambled in butter,
       1 large egg 5

    Chicken, boiled, poached, or scrambled in butter,
       1 medium egg 4

    Chicken, dried, whole, 1 oz. 1.2

    Chicken, raw, white of 1 large egg 3

    Chicken, raw, white of 1 medium egg 2

    Chicken, raw, whole, 1 large 5

    Chicken, raw, whole, 1 medium 4

    Chicken, raw, yolk of 1 large egg 1

    Chicken, raw, yolk of 1 medium egg 1

    Chicken, scrambled, made with milk, cooked in fat,
       1 large egg 1.5

Chicken, scrambled, made with milk, cooked in fat,
1 medium egg 1.3
Duck, raw, 1 egg 5
Elderberries, fresh, with stems, 1 lb. 69.9
Endive
French or Belgian, raw, 1 lb. 12.9
French or Belgian, raw, 1 head (5"–7" long) 1.7
French or Belgian, raw, chopped, 1 cup 2.9
Escarole or curly endive
Raw, 1 lb. 16.4
Raw, cut pieces, 1 cup 2.1

F

	grams
Fat, vegetable shortening or cooking	0
Fennel leaves, raw, untrimmed, 1 lb.	21.5

Figs

Candied, 1 oz.	20.9
Canned, heavy syrup, 3 figs and 1¾ tbsp. liquid ..	18.5
Canned, heavy syrup, with liquid, 1 cup	56.5
Canned, water pack, 3 figs and 1¾ tbsp. liquid ...	9.9
Canned, water pack, with liquid, 1 cup	30.8
Dried, 4 oz.	78.4
Fresh, 1 lb.	92.1
Fresh, 1 large (2½" diameter)	13.2
Fresh, 1 small (1½" diameter)	8.1

Filberts or hazelnuts

Ground, 1 cup	12.5
In shell, 1 lb.	34.9
In shell, 4 oz.	8.7
In shell, 10 nuts	2.3
Shelled, 1 lb.	75.8
Shelled, 4 oz.	19.0

Shelled, chopped, 1 cup 19.2
Shelled, whole, 1 cup 22.5
Finnan haddie 0
Fish (see individual listings)
Fish cakes
Frozen, breaded, fried, 8 oz. 39.0
Frozen, breaded, fried, 1 cake (3" diameter) 10.3
Fish flakes, canned 0
Fish flour 0
Fish sticks
Frozen, breaded, fried, 8 oz. 14.8
Frozen, breaded, fried, 1 stick (4" × 1" × ½") .. 1.8
Flounder 0
Flour
All-purpose, sifted, 1 cup 87.5
Bread, sifted, 1 cup 85.9
Buckwheat, dark, sifted, 1 cup 70.6
Buckwheat, light, sifted, 1 cup 77.9
Cake or pastry, sifted, 1 cup 76.2
Carob (St.-John's-bread), 1 cup 113.0
Corn, unsifted, 1 cup 89.9
Gluten (45%), unsifted, 1 cup 63.7
Rye, dark, unsifted, 1 cup 87.2
Rye, light, sifted, 1 cup 68.6
Soybean, defatted, unsifted, 1 cup 38.1
Wheat, self-rising, sifted, 1 cup 85.3
Frankfurters
1 lb. (8–10 frankfurters) 8.2
4 oz. 2.8

Unsmoked, 1 lb. 11.3
Unsmoked, 1 average (1–3/5 oz.) 1.1
Unsmoked, 1 small (⅓ oz.) 3
Smoked, 1 average (1½ oz.) 1.1
Smoked, 1 small (⅓ oz.) 2
Canned, 4 oz. 2
Canned, 1 average (1.7 oz.) 1
Frostings (see Icing)
Fruit (see individual listings)
Fruit cocktail
Canned, heavy syrup, with liquid, 1 cup 50.2
Canned, water pack, with liquid, 1 cup 23.8
Fruit salad
Canned, heavy syrup, with liquid, 1 cup 49.5
Canned, water pack, with liquid, 1 cup 22.3

G

grams

Garbanzos (see Chickpeas)

Garlic, raw, peeled, 1 average clove 9

Gelatin, unflavored 0

Gelatin dessert, flavored, prepared with water, 1 cup ..33.8

Gin (see Alcoholic Beverages, pages 130–32)

Ginger, candied, 1 oz. 24.7

Ginger ale (see Soft drinks)

Ginger root, fresh, peeled, 1 oz. 2.5

Goat's milk (see Milk)

Goose 0

Gooseberries

    Canned, heavy syrup, with liquid, 4 oz. 26.2

    Canned, water pack, with liquid, 4 oz. 7.4

    Fresh, 1 cup 14.6

Granadilla (see Passion fruit)

Grape drink, canned, 1 cup 34.5

Grape juice

    Canned, 1 cup 42.0

    Frozen, sweetened, diluted, 1 cup 33.3

Grapes

American type (Concord, Delaware, etc.), 1 cup ...15.9
American type (Concord, Delaware, etc.), 1 lb. 44.9
American type (Concord, Delaware, etc.), 10 grapes.4.1
European type (Thompson seedless, etc.), 1 cup ..27.7
European type (Thompson seedless, etc.), 1 lb. ...69.8
European type (Thompson seedless, etc.), 10 grapes.8.7
Canned, heavy syrup, with liquid, 1 cup 51.2
Canned, water pack, with liquid, 1 cup 33.3

Grapefruit

Canned, syrup pack, with liquid, 1 cup 45.2
Canned, water pack, with liquid, 1 cup 18.5
Pink, fresh, sections, 1 cup 20.8
Pink, fresh, sections, 1 cup with 2 tbsp. liquid 23.9
Pink, fresh, seeded, 1 average (4¼" diameter) ..30.1
Pink, fresh, seeded, ½ average (4¼" diameter) ..15.0
Pink, fresh, seedless, 1 average (3¾" diameter) ..25.6
Pink, fresh, seedless, ½ average (3¾" diameter).12.8
White, fresh, sections, 1 cup 20.2
White, fresh, sections, 1 cup with 2 tbsp. liquid ..23.2
White, fresh, seeded, 1 average (4¼" diameter) ..29.3
White, fresh, seeded, ½ average (4¼" diameter)..14.7
White, fresh, seedless, 1 average (3¾" diameter)..23.9
White, fresh, seedless, ½ average (3¾" diameter) 11.9

Grapefruit juice

Canned, sweetened, 1 cup 32.0
Canned, unsweetened, 1 cup 24.2
Dehydrated, crystals with water, 1 cup 23.7
Fresh, pink or white, 1 cup 22.6

Frozen, sweetened, diluted, 1 cup 28.3

Frozen, unsweetened, diluted, 1 cup 24.2

Grapefruit-orange juice

Canned, sweetened, 1 cup 30.4

Canned, unsweetened, 1 cup 24.9

Frozen, unsweetened, diluted, 1 cup 26.0

Grapefruit peel, candied, 1 oz. 22.9

Grits (see Corn grits)

Ground-cherries

Raw, with husk, 1 lb. 46.7

Raw, without husk, 1 cup 15.7

Grouper 0

Guava

Fresh, 1 lb. 66.0

Fresh, strawberry, 1 lb. 70.2

Guinea hen 0

Gum

Chewing, candy-coated, 1 piece

(¾" × ½" × ¼") 1.6

Chewing, sweetened, ½ oz. 18.5

H

	grams
Haddock, fresh or smoked	0
Halibut, fresh or smoked	0
Ham	
Canned, cured, boneless, 1 lb.	4.1
Canned, cured, boneless, 4 oz.	1.0
Canned, deviled	0
Canned, spiced, 4 oz.	1.6
Fresh, boiled or light-cure, all cuts	0
Long-cure, 1 lb.	1.2
Long-cure, 4 oz.	.3
Hash	
Corned beef, with potatoes, canned, 1 cup	23.5
Corned beef, with potatoes, canned, 8 oz.	24.3
Hazelnuts (see Filberts)	
Headcheese	
Packaged, 1 lb.	4.5
Packaged, 4 oz.	1.2
Round, 4 oz.	1.1

Heart

Beef, braised, 4 oz. 8
Beef, braised, chopped or diced, 1 cup 1.0
Calf, braised, 4 oz. 2.0
Calf, braised, chopped or diced, 1 cup 2.6
Chicken, simmered, 4 oz. 1
Chicken, simmered, chopped or diced, 1 cup 1
Hog, braised, 4 oz. 4
Hog, braised, chopped or diced, 1 cup 4
Lamb, braised, 4 oz. 1.2
Lamb, braised, chopped or diced, 1 cup 1.5
Turkey, simmered, 4 oz. 4
Turkey, simmered, chopped or diced, 1 cup 3

Herring

Canned in tomato sauce, with liquid, 4 oz. 4.2
Fresh or canned 0
Pickled, smoked, kippered, salted or brined 0

Hickory nuts

In shell, 1 lb. 20.3
In shell, 4 oz. 5.1
Shelled, 1 lb. 58.1
Shelled, 4 oz. 14.5

Hominy grits (see Corn grits)

Honey

Strained or extracted, 1 cup 279.0
Strained or extracted, 1 tbsp. 17.3
Strained or extracted, 1 oz. 23.3

Honeydew melon

Fresh, 1 melon (6½" diameter) 115.5

Fresh, 1 wedge (2" × 7") ....:...11.5
Fresh, diced, 1 cup 13.1
Fresh, with rind and seeds, 1 lb. 22.0
Frozen, melon balls with cantaloupe, in syrup,
   1 cup 36.1
Horseradish
Fresh, pared, 1 oz. 5.6
Prepared, 1 tbsp. 1.4
Prepared, 1 tsp. 5
Hyacinth beans, mature seeds, dry, 4 oz. 69.5

I

Ice cream
 Hardened (10% fat), ½ gal. 221.3
 Hardened (10% fat), 1 cup 27.7
 Hardened, rich (16% fat), ½ gal. 213.8
 Hardened, rich (16% fat), 1 cup 26.6
 Soft-serve (frozen custard), 1 cup 36.0
Ice milk
 Hardened (5.1% fat), ½ gal. 234.8
 Hardened (5.1% fat), 1 cup 29.3
 Soft-serve (5.1% fat), 1 cup 39.2
Ices, water, flavored, 1 cup 62.9
Icing
 Cake, mix, prepared, chocolate fudge, 1 cup 207.7
 Cake, mix, prepared with water, creamy fudge,
 1 cup 182.8
Inconnu (sheefish), raw 0

J

	grams
Jack mackerel, raw	0
Jackfruit	
Fresh, peeled and seeded, 4 oz.	28.9
Fresh, whole, 1 lb.	32.2
Jams and preserves	
All flavors, 1 lb.	317.4
All flavors, 1 oz.	19.8
All flavors, 1 tbsp.	14.0
Jellies	
All flavors, 1 lb.	320.1
All flavors, 1 oz.	20.0
All flavors, 1 tbsp.	12.7
Jerusalem artichokes	
Pared, 4 oz.	19.0
Whole, with skin, 1 lb.	52.3
Juices (see individual listings)	
Jujube	
Dried, whole, with seeds, 4 oz.	74.3

Dried, without seeds, 4 oz. 83.9
Fresh, whole, 4 oz. 31.5

K

grams

Kale

    Fresh, boiled, drained, leaves, 1 cup 6.7

    Fresh, leaves only, 4 oz. 10.2

    Fresh, whole, with stems, 1 lb. 20.1

    Fresh, whole, without stems, 1 lb. 26.1

    Frozen, boiled, drained, leaves, 1 cup 7.0

Kidney

    Beef, braised, 4 oz. 9

    Beef, braised, pieces or sliced, 1 cup 1.1

    Calf, raw, 4 oz. 1

    Hog, raw, 4 oz. 1.1

    Lamb, raw, 4 oz. 9

Kingfish 0

Kippered herring 0

Knockwurst

    1 lb. 10.0

    4 oz. 2.5

    1 link (4" $\times$ 1⅛" diameter) 1.5

Kohlrabi

    Boiled, drained, diced, 1 cup 8.7

    Raw, without leaves, 1 lb. 21.9

Kumquats

    Fresh, whole, 1 lb. 72.1

    Fresh, 1 medium (about ¾ oz.) 3.2

L

	grams
Ladyfingers (see Cookies)	
Lamb	0
Lamb's-quarters	
Boiled, drained, 4 oz.	5.7
Raw, trimmed, 1 lb.	33.1
Leeks, raw, untrimmed, 1 lb.	26.4
Lemon juice	
Canned or bottled, 1 cup	18.5
Fresh, 1 cup	19.5
Fresh, canned, or frozen, 1 tbsp.	1.2
Frozen, single-strength, 6-oz. can	13.2
Lemon peel	
Candied, 1 oz.	22.9
Raw, grated, 1 tbsp.	1.0
Lemonade	
Frozen, diluted, 1 qt.	111.9
Frozen, diluted, 1 cup	28.3
Lemons	
Fresh, 1 lb.	48.1

Fresh, 1 average lemon (2⅛" diameter) 6.0
Fresh, 1 large lemon (2⅜" diameter) 8.7
Fresh, 1 wedge (¼ average lemon) 1.6

Lentils
Split, uncooked, 1 cup 117.4
Whole, dried, 1 cup 114.2
Whole, cooked, 1 cup 38.6

Lettuce
Boston or bibb, 1 head (5" diameter) 4.1
Boston or bibb, 2 inner (medium) leaves 4
Boston or bibb, chopped or shredded, 1 cup 1.4
Boston or bibb, untrimmed, 1 lb. 8.4
Iceberg, 1 head (6" diameter) 15.6
Iceberg, ¼ head (6" diameter head) 3.9
Iceberg, 1 leaf (5" × 4½") 6
Iceberg, shredded pieces, 1 cup 1.6
Iceberg, untrimmed, 1 lb. 12.5
Romaine, shredded pieces, 1 cup 1.9
Romaine, untrimmed, 1 lb. 10.2
Simpson or looseleaf, shredded pieces, 1 cup 1.9
Simpson or looseleaf, untrimmed, 1 lb. 10.2

Lichee nuts
Dried, 4 oz. 36.9
Raw, in shell, 4 oz. 11.2
Raw, shelled, 4 oz. 18.0

Lima beans (see Beans)

Lime juice
Fresh, canned, or bottled, unsweetened, 1 cup 22.1
Fresh, canned, or bottled, unsweetened, 1 tbsp. 1.4

Fresh, canned, or bottled, unsweetened, 1 oz. 2.8

Limeade

Frozen, diluted, 1 qt. 107.9

Frozen, diluted, 1 cup 27.0

Limes

Fresh, 1 lb. 36.2

Fresh, 1 average lime (2″ diameter) 6.4

Liver

Beef, fried, 1 lb. 24.0

Beef, fried, 4 oz. 6.0

Calf, fried, 1 lb. 18.1

Calf, fried, 4 oz. 4.6

Chicken or turkey, simmered, 1 lb. 14.1

Chicken or turkey, simmered, 4 oz. 3.5

Chicken or turkey, simmered, chopped, 1 cup 4.3

Hog, fried, 1 lb. 11.3

Hog, fried, 4 oz. 2.9

Lamb, broiled, 1 lb. 12.7

Lamb, broiled, 4 oz. 3.2

Liver paste (see Pate de foie gras)

Liverwurst

Fresh, 1 lb. 8.2

Fresh, 4 oz. 2.1

Smoked, 1 lb. 10.4

Smoked, 4 oz. 2.6

Lobster

Cooked or canned, meat only, 1 cup.............4

Cooked or canned, meat only, 1 lb. 1.4

Cooked or canned, meat only, 4 oz. 4

Lobster paste
    1 oz. 4
    1 tsp. 1
Loganberries
    Canned, heavy syrup, with liquid, 4 oz. 25.3
    Canned, juice pack, with liquid, 4 oz. 14.5
    Canned, water pack, with liquid, 4 oz. 10.7
    Fresh, trimmed, 1 cup 21.5
    Fresh, untrimmed, 1 lb. 67.6
Loquats
    Fresh, 10 fruits 15.3
    Fresh, whole, 1 lb. 43.3
Lychees, raw, 10 fruits 14.8

M

	grams
Macadamia nuts	
Shelled, 1 lb.	72.1
Shelled, 4 oz.	18.0
Macaroni	
Boiled 8–10 minutes, drained, 1 cup	39.1
Boiled 14–20 minutes, drained, 1 cup	32.2
Macaroni and cheese	
Canned, 1 cup	25.7
Canned, 4 oz.	12.1
Mackerel, fresh, canned, or salted	0
Malt, dried, 1 oz.	21.9
Malt extract, dried, 1 oz.	25.3
Mangos	
Fresh, diced or sliced, 1 cup	27.7
Fresh, whole, 1 lb.	51.1
Fresh, whole, 1 average (1½ per lb.)	38.8
Margarine, salted or unsalted	
Regular or whipped, 1 lb.	1.8
Regular, 1 cup (2 sticks, or ½ lb.)	.9

Regular, 1 stick (¼ lb., or 8 tbsp.) 5

Regular, 1 tbsp. 1

Regular, 1 pat ....tr.

Whipped, 1 cup 6

Whipped, 1 tbsp. ....tr.

Whipped, 1 pat ....tr.

Marmalade

Citrus flavors, 1 lb. 318.0

Citrus flavors, 1 oz. 19.9

Citrus flavors, 1 tbsp. 14.0

Marmalade plums, fresh, whole, 1 lb. 108.9

Matai (see Water chestnuts)

Mayonnaise (see Salad dressings)

Meat (see individual listings)

Meat loaf (luncheon meat)

1 lb. 15.0

4 oz. 3.8

Melon (see individual listings)

Melon balls, frozen, in syrup, 4 oz. 17.8

Milk

Cow's, buttermilk, cultured, 1 cup 12.5

Cow's, chocolate-flavored, skim, canned, 1 qt. ...109.0

Cow's, chocolate-flavored, skim, canned, 1 cup ...27.3

Cow's, chocolate-flavored, whole, canned, 1 qt. ..110.0

Cow's, chocolate-flavored, whole, canned, 1 cup ..27.5

Cow's, canned, condensed, sweetened, 1 cup 166.2

Cow's, canned, condensed, sweetened, 1 fl. oz. 20.7

Cow's, canned, evaporated, unsweetened, 1 cup ..24.4

Cow's, canned, evaporated, unsweetened, 1 fl. oz. ..3.1

Cow's, dried, nonfat, instant, 1 envelope (3.2 oz.). .47.0
Cow's, dried, whole, dry form, ½ cup 24.5
Cow's, skim, 1 qt. 50.0
Cow's, skim, 1 cup 12.5
Cow's, skim, low-fat, 1 cup 14.8
Cow's, whole (3.5% fat), 1 qt. 47.8
Cow's, whole (3.5% fat), 1 cup 12.0
Goat's, whole, 1 cup 11.2
Malted, beverage, 1 cup 27.5
Malted, powder, 1 oz. (3 heaping tsp.) 20.1
Mixed vegetables (see Vegetables, mixed)
Molasses (see Syrups)
Mortadella
   1 lb. 2.7
   4 oz. 8
Muffin, corn, mix, made with egg and milk, 1.4 oz. 20.0
Mullet 0
Mushrooms
   Canned, with liquid, 4 oz. 2.7
   Raw, untrimmed, 1 lb. 19.4
   Raw, trimmed, sliced, diced, or chopped, 1 cup ...3.1
Muskmelon (see Honeydew melon)
Mussels
   Canned, drained, meat only, 4 oz. 1.7
   Raw, in shell, 1 lb. 7.2
   Raw, meat only, 4 oz. 3.8
Mustard, prepared, brown or yellow, 1 tsp. 3
Mustard greens
   Boiled, drained, 1 cup 5.6

Frozen, chopped, boiled, drained, 1 cup 4.7
Raw, untrimmed, 1 lb. 17.8
Mustard spinach
    Boiled, drained, 1 cup 5.0
    Raw, 1 lb. 17.7

N

Nectarines

    Fresh, 1 average (2½″ diameter) 23.6

    Fresh, whole, 1 lb. 71.4

New Zealand spinach (see Spinach, New Zealand)

Noodles

    Chow-mein type, canned, 1 cup 26.1

    Chow-mein type, canned, 5-oz. can 82.4

    Egg, cooked, 1 cup 37.3

    Egg, cooked, 1 lb. 105.7

Nuts (see individual listings)

O

Oats, Oatmeal (see Cereal)

Ocean perch

    Frozen, breaded, fried, 4 oz. 18.8

    Raw 0

Octopus 0

Oil

    Salad or cooking 0

    Olive 0

Okra

    Boiled, drained, 10 pods (3" long) 6.4

    Boiled, drained, crosscut slices, 1 cup 9.6

    Frozen, cuts, boiled, drained, 1 cup 16.3

    Raw, crosscut slices, 1 cup 7.6

    Raw, untrimmed, 1 lb. 29.6

Oleomargarine (see Margarine)

Olive oil (see Oil)

Olives, pickled, canned, or bottled

    Green, 10 giant olives (7/8" diameter) 9

    Green, 10 large olives (3/4" diameter) 5

Green, pitted, 1 lb. 5.9
Ripe, Ascolano, 10 extra large olives (¾" diameter) 1.2
Ripe, Ascolano, pitted, 1 lb. 11.8
Ripe, Ascolano, sliced, 1 cup 3.5
Ripe, Manzanilla, pitted, 1 lb. 11.8
Ripe, Manzanilla or Mission, 10 large olives
  (¾" diameter) 1.2
Ripe, Manzanilla or Mission, sliced, 1 cup 3.9
Ripe, Mission, pitted, 1 lb. 14.5
Ripe, salt-cured, Greek-style, 10 extra large olives ..2.3
Ripe, salt-cured, Greek-style, pitted, 1 lb. 39.5
Onions
Dehydrated, 1 oz. 23.3
Green, bulb and white portion, 2 medium scallions
  (⅝" diameter) 3.2
Green, bulb and white portion, 6 small scallions
  (⅜" diameter) 3.2
Green, bulb and white portion, chopped, 1 cup ...10.5
Green, bulb and white portion, chopped, 1 tbsp. 6
Green, tops (green portion), chopped, 1 cup 5.5
Green, tops (green portion), chopped, 1 tbsp. 3
Green, whole, untrimmed, 1 lb. 35.7
Mature, boiled, drained, whole or sliced, 1 cup ...13.7
Mature, raw, chopped, 1 cup 14.8
Mature, raw, chopped, 1 tbsp. 9
Mature, raw, chopped, 4 oz. 7.4
Mature, raw, grated, 1 cup 20.4
Mature, raw, sliced, 1 cup 10.0
Mature, raw, untrimmed, 1 lb. 35.9

Mature, raw, whole, 1 average onion
(2½" diameter) 8.8
Orange juice
Canned, sweetened, 1 cup 30.5
Canned, sweetened, 1 fl. oz. 3.8
Canned, unsweetened, 1 cup 27.9
Canned, unsweetened, 1 fl. oz. 3.5
Dehydrated, crystals with water, 1 cup 26.8
Frozen, unsweetened, diluted with water, 1 qt. ...115.4
Frozen, unsweetened, diluted with water, 1 cup ...28.9
Fresh, California, navel, 1 cup 28.1
Fresh, California, Valencia, 1 cup 26.0
Fresh, Florida, early season and midseason, 1 cup.22.9
Fresh, Florida, Valencia, 1 cup 26.0
Fresh, Florida, Temple, 1 cup 32.0
Orange peel
Candied, 1 oz. 22.9
Raw, grated, 1 oz. 7.1
Raw, grated, 1 tbsp. 1.5
Orange-apricot juice drink, canned, 1 cup 31.6
Orange-cranberry relish (see Cranberry relish with orange)
Orange-grapefruit juice (see Grapefruit-orange juice)
Oranges, fresh
Florida, all varieties, whole, 1 lb. 40.3
Florida, all varieties, 1 average orange
(2⅝" diameter) 16.9
Florida, all varieties, 1 small orange
(2½" diameter) 14.5
Florida, all varieties, 1 slice (¼" × 2½") 2.5

Navel, whole, 1 lb. 39.2

Navel, 1 average orange (2⅞″ diameter) 17.8

Navel, 1 small orange (2⅜″ diameter) 11.3

Navel, 1 slice (¼″ × 2½″) 2.7

Sections, diced, 1 cup 25.6

Sections, without membranes, 1 cup 22.0

Valencia, 1 average orange (2⅝″ diameter) 15.0

Valencia, 1 small orange (2⅜″ diameter) 12.2

Valencia, 1 slice (¼″ × 2″) 1.9

Oysters, raw

Eastern, 2 medium or 3 small oysters 1.0

Eastern, in shell, 1 lb. 1.5

Eastern, meat only, 4 oz. 3.9

Eastern, meat only, whole, 1 cup 8.2

Pacific or western, 4–6 medium or
6–9 small oysters 15.5

Pacific or western, meat only, 4 oz. 7.3

P

Pancakes, mix, prepared as directed

 Buckwheat and other flours, 1 cake (6″ diameter). 17.4

 Buckwheat and other flours, 1 cake (4″ diameter). . 6.4

 Plain or buttermilk, 1 cake (6″ diameter) 23.7

 Plain or buttermilk, 1 cake (4″ diameter) 8.7

Papayas

 Cubed (½″ pieces), 1 cup .14.0

 Mashed, 1 cup 23.0

 Whole, 1 papaya (3½″ × 5⅛″, 1 lb.) 30.4

Parsley

 Chopped, 1 cup 5.1

 Chopped, 1 tbsp. 3

 Whole, 1 lb. 38.6

 Whole, 10 sprigs (2½″ long) 9

Parsnips

 Boiled, drained, 1 large parsnip (9″ × 2¼″) 23.8

 Boiled, drained, 1 small parsnip (6″ × 1⅛″) 5.2

 Boiled, drained, diced, 1 cup 23.1

 Boiled, drained, mashed, 1 cup 31.3

Raw, whole, 1 lb. 67.5
Passion fruit, fresh, 1 lb. 50.0
Pastina
    Egg, dried, 1 cup 122.1
    Egg, dried, 4 oz. 81.4
Pastry shell (see Pie crust)
Pate de foie gras
    Canned, 1 oz. 1.4
    Canned, 1 tbsp. 6
    Canned, 1 tsp. 2
Pawpaws, North American type
    Mashed, 1 cup 42.0
    Whole, 1 lb. 57.2
    Whole, 1 pawpaw (2" diameter) 16.4
Peach nectar
    Canned, 1 oz. 3.9
    Canned, 1 cup 30.9
Peaches
    Canned, heavy syrup, 1 peach half with
      2½ tbsp. syrup 21.9
    Canned, heavy syrup, with liquid, 1 cup 51.5
    Canned, juice pack, 4 oz. 13.2
    Canned, water pack, 1 lb. 36.7
    Canned, water pack, 4 oz. 9.2
    Canned, water pack, with liquid, 1 cup 19.8
    Dehydrated, uncooked, 1 cup 88.0
    Dried, 4 oz. 77.5
    Dried, halves, 1 cup 109.3
    Dried, halves, 1 lb..........................309.8

Dried, 10 large halves 99.0
Dried, 10 medium halves 88.8
Dried, cooked, sweetened, with liquid, 1 cup 83.2
Dried, cooked, unsweetened, with liquid, 1 cup ... 53.5
Fresh, 1 large peach (2¾" diameter) 14.8
Fresh, 1 medium peach (2½" diameter) 9.7
Fresh, pared, 1 lb. 33.4
Fresh, pared, 1 large peach (2¾" diameter) 12.9
Fresh, pared, 1 medium peach (2½" diameter) 8.5
Fresh, pared, diced, 1 cup 17.9
Fresh, pared, sliced, 1 cup 16.5
Fresh, whole, 1 lb. 38.3
Frozen, sliced, sweetened, 1 cup 56.5

Peanut butter
  1 cup 48.5
  1 tbsp. 3.0
  1 oz. 5.3
Peanut spread, 1 oz. 6.3
Peanuts
  Raw, in shell, 1 lb. 18.6
  Raw, in shell, 4 oz. 15.4
  Raw, shelled, 1 lb. 17.6
  Raw, shelled, 4 oz. 21.1
  Roasted, in shell, 1 lb. 20.6
  Roasted, in shell, 4 oz. 15.7
  Roasted, in shell, 10 jumbo nuts 3.7
  Roasted, shelled, 1 cup 27.1
  Roasted, shelled, 1 lb. 93.4
  Roasted, shelled, 4 oz. 23.4

Roasted, chopped. 1 cup 29.7
Roasted, chopped. 1 tbsp. 1.9
Spanish type, roasted. salted, 1 cup 27.1
Spanish type, roasted, salted, 1 lb. 85.3
Spanish type. roasted, salted, chopped, 1 tbsp. 1.7
Pear, prickly (see Prickly pear)
Pear nectar
    Canned, 1 cup 33.0
    Canned, 1 fl. oz. 4.1
Pears
    Candied, 1 oz. 21.5
    Canned, heavy syrup, with liquid, 1 cup 50.0
    Canned, heavy syrup, with liquid, 1 lb. 88.9
    Canned, heavy syrup, 1 pear half with 2 tbsp. syrup 18.4
    Canned, water pack, with liquid, 1 cup 20.3
    Canned, water pack, with liquid, 1 lb. 37.6
    Canned, water pack, 1 pear half with 2 tbsp. liquid. .7.6
    Dried, 4 oz. 76.4
    Dried, cooked, sweetened, with liquid, 1 cup 106.4
    Dried, cooked, unsweetened, with liquid, 1 cup 80.8
    Dried, halves, 1 cup 121.1
    Dried, halves, 1 lb. 305.3
    Dried, 10 halves 117.8
    Fresh, Bartlett, 1 pear (2½″ diameter) 25.1
    Fresh, Bosc, 1 pear (2½″ diameter) 21.6
    Fresh, D'Anjou, 1 pear (3″ diameter) 30.6
    Fresh, sliced, 1 cup 25.2
    Fresh, whole, 1 lb. 63.2

Peas

Black-eyed (see Cowpeas)

Green, canned, early or June, drained, 1 cup 28.6

Green, canned, early or June, drained, 1 lb. 76.2

Green, canned, early or June, with liquid, 1 cup .. 31.1

Green, canned, early or June, with liquid, 1 lb. ... 56.7

Green, canned, sweet, drained, 1 cup 25.5

Green, canned, sweet, drained, 1 lb. 68.0

Green, canned, sweet, with liquid, 1 cup 25.9

Green, canned, sweet, with liquid, 1 lb. 47.2

Green, fresh, boiled, drained, 1 cup 19.4

Green, fresh, boiled, drained, 1 lb. 54.9

Green, fresh, in pods, 1 lb. 24.8

Green, fresh, raw, 1 cup 20.9

Green, fresh, raw, 1 lb. 65.3

Green, frozen, boiled, drained, 1 cup 18.9

Green, frozen, boiled, drained, 1 lb. 53.5

Split, cooked, 1 cup 41.6

Split, cooked, 1 lb. 94.3

Split, uncooked, 1 cup 125.4

Peas and carrots

Frozen, boiled, drained, 1 cup 16.2

Frozen, boiled, drained, 1 lb. 45.8

Pecans

In shell, 1 lb. 35.1

In shell, 4 oz. 8.8

In shell, 10 large nuts 5.0

Shelled, 1 lb. 66.2

Shelled, 4 oz. 16.6

Shelled, chopped, 1 cup 17.2
Shelled, chopped, 1 tbsp. 1.1
Shelled, ground, 1 cup 13.9
Shelled, halves, 1 cup 15.8
Shelled, halves, 10 large nuts 1.3
Pepper, black, ½ tsp. 5
Peppers
Hot chili, green, canned, chili sauce, 1 cup 12.3
Hot chili, green, canned, pods, with liquid, 4 oz. ..6.9
Hot chili, green, raw, seeded, 4 oz. 10.4
Hot chili, green, raw, whole, 1 lb. 30.1
Hot chili, red, canned, chili sauce, 1 cup 9.6
Hot chili, red, dried, chili powder, seasoned, 1 tsp. 1.1
Hot chili, red, raw, pods, seeded, 4 oz. 18.0
Hot chili, red, raw, whole, 1 lb. 78.8
Sweet green, boiled, drained, 1 lb. 17.2
Sweet green, boiled, drained, strips, 1 cup 5.1
Sweet green, fancy grade, boiled, drained,
    1 pepper (3″ diameter) 6.1
Sweet green, fancy grade, raw, 1 pepper
    (3″ diameter) 7.9
Sweet green, #1 grade, boiled, drained,
    1 pepper (2½″ diameter) 2.8
Sweet green, #1 grade, raw, 1 pepper
    (2½″ diameter) 3.5
Sweet green, raw, 1 ring (3″ diameter) 5
Sweet green, raw, chopped or diced, 1 cup 7.2
Sweet green, raw, sliced, 1 cup 3.8
Sweet green, raw, strips, 1 cup 4.8

Sweet green, raw, whole, 1 lb. 17.9

Sweet red, fancy grade, raw, 1 pepper
    (3″ diameter) 11.6

Sweet red, #1 grade, raw, 1 pepper
    (2½″ diameter) 5.2

Sweet red, raw, 1 ring (3″ diameter) 4

Sweet red, raw, chopped or diced, 1 cup 10.7

Sweet red, raw, sliced, 1 cup 5.7

Sweet red, raw, strips, 1 cup 7.1

Sweet red, raw, whole, 1 lb. 25.8

Perch 0

Persimmons

Japanese or kaki, seedless, 1 lb. 75.1

Japanese or kaki, seedless, 1 average persimmon
    (2½″ diameter) 33.1

Japanese or kaki, with seeds, 1 lb. 73.3

Native, 1 lb. 124.6

Native, 1 average persimmon (2½″ diameter) 8.2

Pickle relish

Sweet, 1 cup 83.3

Sweet, 1 tbsp. 5.1

Pickles

Cucumber, dill, 4 oz. 2.5

Cucumber, dill, 1 large pickle (4″ long) 3.0

Cucumber, dill, 1 medium pickle (3¾″ long) 1.4

Cucumber, dill, crosscut slices, 1 cup 3.4

Cucumber, dill, 2 crosscut slices (1½″ diameter) .. .3

Cucumber, fresh, bread and butter, 4 oz. 20.4

Cucumber, fresh, bread and butter, crosscut slices,
  1 cup 30.4
Cucumber, fresh, bread and butter, 2 crosscut slices
  (1½" diameter) 2.7
Cucumber, sour, 4 oz. 2.3
Cucumber, sour, 1 large pickle (4" long) 2.7
Cucumber, sour, 1 medium pickle (3¾" long) 1.3
Cucumber, sweet, 4 oz. 41.6
Cucumber, sweet, chopped, 1 cup 58.4
Cucumber, sweet, sliced lengthwise, 1 spear
  (4¼" long) 7.3
Cucumber, sweet gherkins, 1 large pickle (3" long) 12.8
Cucumber, sweet gherkins, 1 small pickle
  (2½" long) 5.5
Mustard (chow-chow), sour, 1 cup 9.8
Mustard (chow-chow), sweet, 1 cup 66.2
Pie
  Apple, frozen, baked, 1 whole pie (8" diameter)..219.1
  Apple, frozen, baked, 4⅛" arc (⅙ of 8" pie) 36.5
  Apple, frozen, baked, 3⅛" arc (⅛ of 8" pie) 27.4
  Cherry, frozen, baked, 1 whole pie (8" diameter) 257.4
  Cherry, frozen, baked, 4⅛" arc (⅙ of 8" pie) ...42.9
  Cherry, frozen, baked, 3⅛" arc (⅛ of 8" pie) ...32.2
  Coconut custard, frozen, baked, 1 whole pie
    (8" diameter) 177.0
  Coconut custard, frozen, baked, 4⅛" arc
    (⅙ of 8" pie) 29.5
  Coconut custard, frozen, baked, 3⅛" arc
    (⅛ of 8" pie) 22.1

Coconut custard, mix, made with egg yolks and milk, baked, 1 whole pie (8″ diameter) 231.9

Coconut custard, mix, made with egg yolks and milk, baked, 4⅛″ arc (⅙ of 8″ pie) 38.7

Coconut custard, mix, made with egg yolks and milk, baked, 3⅛″ arc (⅛ of 8″ pie) 29.1

Pie crust, mix, baked, yield from 10-oz. package 140.8

Pigeon peas, dry, 4 oz. 72.6

Pignolias (see Pine nuts)

Pig's feet, pickled 0

Pike 0

Pili nuts

    In shell, 1 lb. 6.9

    In shell, 4 oz. 1.7

    Shelled, 1 lb. 38.1

    Shelled, 4 oz. 9.6

Pimientos

    Canned, with liquid, 1 lb. 26.3

    Canned, with liquid, 4 oz. 6.6

Pine nuts

    Pignolias, shelled, 1 lb. 52.6

    Pignolias, shelled, 4 oz. 13.2

    Pinon, in shell, 1 lb. 53.9

    Pinon, in shell, 4 oz. 13.5

    Pinon, shelled, 1 lb. 93.0

    Pinon, shelled, 4 oz. 23.2

Pineapple

    Candied, 1 oz. 22.7

    Candied, 2 slices or ½ cup chunks 90.4

Canned, extra heavy syrup, with liquid, 4 oz. 26.5
Canned, heavy syrup, 1 large slice and
   2¼ tbsp. syrup 20.4
Canned, heavy syrup, chunks or crushed, 1 cup ...49.5
Canned, heavy syrup, with liquid, 4 oz. 22.0
Canned, juice pack, with liquid, 4 oz. 17.1
Canned, tidbits, water pack, with liquid, 1 cup 25.1
Canned, water pack, with liquid, 4 oz. 11.6
Fresh, 1 slice (3½" diameter × ¾") 11.5
Fresh, diced, 1 cup 21.2
Fresh, whole, untrimmed, 1 lb. 32.3
Frozen, chunks, sweetened, 1 cup 54.4

Pineapple juice
Canned, unsweetened, 1 cup 33.8
Canned, unsweetened, 1 fl. oz. 4.2
Frozen, unsweetened, diluted, 1 cup 32.0
Frozen, unsweetened, diluted, 1 fl. oz. 4.0

Pineapple-grapefruit juice drink
Canned, 1 cup 34.0
Canned, 1 fl. oz. 4.3

Pineapple-orange juice drink
Canned, 1 cup 33.8
Canned, 1 fl. oz. 4.2

Pistachio nuts
In shell, 1 lb. 43.1
In shell, 4 oz. 10.8
Shelled, 1 cup 23.7
Shelled, 1 lb. 86.2
Shelled, 4 oz. 21.6

Pitanga

Fresh, pitted, 1 cup 21.3
Fresh, whole, 1 lb. 45.9
Fresh, whole, 2 average fruits 1.2

Pizza, cheese

Frozen, 1 whole pie (10″ diameter) 140.7
Frozen, 1 whole small pie (5¼″ diameter) 25.8
Frozen, 4½″ arc (⅐ of 10″ pie) 20.1

Plantain (see Bananas)

Plums

Damson, fresh, pitted, halves, 1 cup 30.3
Damson, fresh, whole, 1 cup 23.5
Damson, fresh, whole, 1 lb. 73.5
Damson, fresh, whole, 10 plums (1″ diameter) ...17.8
Japanese or hybrid, fresh, pitted, halves, 1 cup ...22.8
Japanese or hybrid, fresh, pitted, sliced or diced,
  1 cup 20.3
Japanese or hybrid, fresh, whole, 1 lb. 52.4
Japanese or hybrid, fresh, whole, 1 plum
  (2⅛″ diameter) 8.1
Prune-type, fresh, pitted, halves, 1 cup 32.5
Prune-type, fresh, whole, 1 lb. 84.0
Prune-type, fresh, whole, 1 plum (1½″ diameter) ..5.6
Purple, canned, whole, heavy syrup, 3 plums and
  2¾ tbsp. syrup 28.7
Purple, canned, whole, heavy syrup, with liquid,
  1 cup 55.8
Purple, canned, whole, heavy syrup, with liquid,
  4 oz. 23.3

Purple, canned, whole, water pack, 3 plums
and 2 tbsp. liquid. 11.3
Purple, canned, whole, water pack, with liquid,
1 cup 29.6
Purple, canned, whole, water pack, with liquid,
4 oz. 12.8
Poha (see Ground-cherries)
Pokeberry shoots, boiled, drained, 1 cup 5.1
Pollock, raw 0
Pomegranates
Fresh, whole, 1 lb. 41.7
Fresh, whole, 1 average pomegranate
(3⅜" diameter) 25.3
Pompano 0
Popcorn
Popped, plain, 1 cup 4.6
Popped, plain, 4 oz. 87.0
Popped, sugar-coated, 1 cup 29.9
Popped, with oil and salt, 1 cup 5.3
Unpopped, 4 oz. 81.8
Pork
Canned, cured, 1 lb. 4.1
Fresh or light-cured 0
Long-cured, country style, 1 lb. 1.2
Pork liver (see Liver, hog)
Pork sausage (see Sausages)
Potato chips
1 oz. 14.2
10 chips (2" diameter) 10.0

Potato sticks
  1 cup 17.8
  1 oz. 14.4
Potatoes
  Sweet, baked in skin, 1 average potato
    (5" long × 2") 37.0
  Sweet, boiled in skin, 1 average potato
    (5" long × 2") 39.8
  Sweet, boiled in skin, mashed, 1 cup 67.1
  Sweet, candied, 4 oz. 38.8
  Sweet, candied, 1 piece (2½" long × 2") 35.9
  Sweet, canned, in syrup, 4 oz. 31.2
  Sweet, canned, vacuum or solid pack, 4 oz. 28.2
  Sweet, canned, vacuum or solid pack, mashed,
    1 cup 63.5
  Sweet, canned, vacuum or solid pack, pieces,
    1 cup 49.8
  Sweet, canned, vacuum or solid pack, pieces,
    1 piece (2¾" long) 10.0
  Sweet, dehydrated flakes, dry form, 1 cup 108.0
  Sweet, dehydrated flakes, with water, 1 cup 57.6
  Sweet, raw, peeled, 1 average potato
    (5" long × 2") 42.6
  Sweet, raw, whole, 1 lb. 96.6
  White, baked in skin, 1 long potato (2⅓" diameter
    × 4¾" long) 32.8
  White, boiled, peeled, 1 lb. 65.8
  White, boiled, peeled, 1 long potato (2⅓" diameter
    × 4¾" long) 32.6

White, boiled, peeled, diced or sliced, 1 cup 22.5
White, boiled, peeled, sliced, 1 round
    (2½" diameter) 19.6
White, boiled in skin, 1 long potato (2⅓" diameter
    × 4¾" long) 38.9
White, boiled in skin, diced or sliced, 1 cup 26.5
White, boiled in skin, sliced, 1 round
    (2½" diameter) 23.3
White, canned, with liquid, 4 oz. 11.2
White, dehydrated flakes, dry form, 1 cup 37.8
White, dehydrated flakes, with water, milk, and
    butter, 1 cup 30.5
White, dehydrated granules, dry form, 1 cup 160.8
White, dehydrated granules, with water, milk, and
    butter, 1 cup 30.2
White, French fried, 10 strips (2"–3½" long) 18.0
White, French fried, 10 strips (1"–2" long) 12.6
White, French fried, frozen, oven-heated, 10 strips
    (2" long) 16.9
White, fried, 1 cup 55.4
White, hash brown, frozen, cooked, 1 cup 45.0
White, mashed, with milk, 1 cup 27.3
White, mashed, with milk and butter, 1 cup 25.8
White, raw, peeled, chopped, diced, or sliced, 1 cup 25.7
White, raw, sliced, 1 round (2½" diameter) 19.2
White, raw, whole, 1 lb. 62.8
White, raw, whole, 1 long potato (2⅓" diameter
    × 4¾") 32.1

Pretzels, commercial varieties

All types, 1 oz. 21.5

Logs, 10 pretzels (3" long) 38.0

Rods, 1 pretzel (7½" long) 10.6

Sticks, 10 pretzels (3⅛" long) 4.6

Sticks, 10 pretzels (2¼" long) 2.3

Twisted, Dutch, 1 pretzel 12.1

Twisted, 1-ring, 10 pretzels 15.2

Twisted, 3-ring, 10 pretzels 22.8

Twisted, thins, 10 pretzels 45.5

Prickly pear

Raw, peeled and seeded, 4 oz. 12.4

Raw, whole, 1 lb. 21.8

Prune juice

Canned, 1 cup 48.6

Canned, 1 fl. oz. 6.1

Prunes

Dehydrated, 1 cup 91.3

Dehydrated (nugget type), 4 oz. 103.5

Dehydrated, cooked, sweetened, with liquid, 1 cup 131.9

Dried, 1 large prune 5.7

Dried, 1 medium prune 4.4

Dried, chopped or ground, not packed, 1 cup 107.8

Dried, with pits, cooked, sweetened, with liquid,
1 cup 107.3

Dried, with pits, cooked, unsweetened, with liquid,
1 cup 66.7

Dried (softenized) pitted, 4 oz. 76.4

Dried (softenized), whole, 10 average prunes 72.4

Pudding, starch base, mix
    Chocolate, cooked with milk, 1 cup 59.3
    Chocolate, instant no-cook, made with milk, 1 cup 63.4
Pumpkin
    Canned, 1 cup 19.4
    Fresh, pulp only, 4 oz. 7.4
    Fresh, whole, 1 lb. 20.6
Pumpkin seeds
    Dried, hulled, 1 cup 21.0
    Dried, hulled, 4 oz. 17.0
Purslane, raw, leaves and stems, 4 oz. 4.3

                                                 grams
Quail 0
Quince
    Fresh, pulp only, 4 oz. 17.4
    Fresh, whole, 1 lb. 42.3

R

	grams
Rabbit	0
Radishes	
Domestic, raw, 10 large radishes (over 1" diameter)	2.9
Domestic, raw, 10 medium radishes (¾"–1" diameter)	1.6
Domestic, raw, sliced, 1 cup	4.1
Domestic, raw, trimmed, 1 lb.	16.3
Domestic, raw, with tops, 1 lb.	10.3
Oriental, raw, pared, 4 oz.	4.8
Oriental, raw, whole, without tops, 1 lb.	14.9
Raisins, seedless	
1 lb.	351.1
4 oz.	87.8
Chopped, firmly packed, 1 cup	147.1
Chopped, loosely packed, 1 cup	104.5
Cooked, sweetened, with liquid, 1 cup	166.4
Ground, firmly packed, 1 cup	209.0
Whole, 1 tbsp.	7.0
Whole, firmly packed, 1 cup	127.7

Whole, loosely packed, 1 cup 112.2

Raspberries

Black, fresh, 1 cup 21.0

Black, fresh, 1 lb. 71.2

Red, canned, water pack, with liquid, 1 cup 21.4

Red, canned, water pack, with liquid, 4 oz. 10.0

Red, fresh, 1 cup 16.7

Red, fresh, 1 lb. 61.7

Red, frozen, sweetened, 1 cup 61.5

Red and gray snapper 0

Redfish (see Ocean perch)

Rhubarb

Cooked, sweetened, 1 cup 97.2

Frozen, cooked, sweetened, 1 cup 97.7

Raw, diced, 1 cup 4.5

Raw, trimmed, 1 lb. 14.4

Raw, with leaves, 1 lb. 7.6

Rice, cooked (hot)

Brown, long-grain, 1 cup 49.7

White, long-grain, 1 cup 49.6

White, long-grain, parboiled, 1 cup 40.8

White, precooked (instant), fluffed, 1 cup 39.9

Rice polish, stirred, spooned into cup, 1 cup 60.6

Rockfish, steamed, with onion, 1 oz. 5

Rolls and buns

Commercial (ready to serve), Cloverleaf, 1-oz. roll
(2½" diameter) 14.8

Commercial (ready to serve), Dinner or pan rolls,
1-oz. roll (2" square) 14.8

Commercial (ready to serve), Frankfurter or
hamburger, 1.4-oz. roll 21.2
Commercial (ready to serve), Hard, rectangular,
⅞"-oz. roll 14.9
Commercial (ready to serve), Hard, round or kaiser,
1¾-oz. roll (3½" diameter) 29.8
Commercial (ready to serve), Hoagie (11½" long
× 3" wide), 1 roll 74.8
Commercial (ready to serve), Raisin, 1-oz. roll ...16.0
Commercial (ready to serve), Sweet, 1-oz. roll 14.0
Commercial (ready to serve), Whole wheat,
1-oz. roll 14.8
Mix, baked, made with water, 1 oz. 15.4
Romaine (see Lettuce)
Root beer (see Soft drinks)
Rose apples, raw, whole, 1 lb. 43.2
Rum (see Alcoholic Beverages, pages 130–32)
Rusk, 1 average loaf (3⅜" diameter) 6.4
Rutabagas
Boiled, drained, cubed, 1 cup 13.9
Boiled, drained, mashed, 1 cup 19.7
Raw, cubed, 1 cup 15.4
Raw, without tops, 1 lb. 42.4
Rye flour (see Flour)

S

	grams
Sablefish	0
Safflower seed kernels, dry, 1 oz.	3.5
Salad dressings, commercial	
Blue cheese, 1 cup	18.1
Blue cheese, 1 tbsp.	1.1
French, 1 cup	43.8
French, 1 tbsp.	2.8
Italian, 1 cup	16.2
Italian, 1 tbsp.	1.0
Mayonnaise, 1 cup	4.8
Mayonnaise, 1 tbsp.	.3
Roquefort cheese, 1 cup	18.1
Roquefort cheese, 1 tbsp.	1.1
Russian, 1 cup	25.5
Russian, 1 tbsp.	1.6
Salad dressing (mayonnaise type), 1 cup	33.8
Salad dressing (mayonnaise type), 1 tbsp.	2.2
Thousand island, 1 cup	38.5
Thousand island, 1 tbsp.	2.5

Salad oil (see Oil)
Salami
    Cooked, 1 lb. 6.4
    Cooked, 4 oz. 1.6
    Cooked, 1 slice (4″ diameter) 3
    Dried, 1 lb. 5.4
    Dried, 4 oz. 1.4
    Dried, 1 slice (3⅛″ diameter) 1
Salmon, fresh, smoked, or canned 0
Salsify
    Freshly harvested, raw, trimmed, 1 lb. 71.0
    Boiled, drained, cubed, 1 cup 20.4
Salt, table 0
Sandwich spread relish
    1 cup 39.0
    1 tbsp. 2.4
    1 oz. 4.5
Sandwiches (about 2-oz. filling on 2 average slices
   white bread [firm-crumb] with 1 tbsp. butter or
   margarine, except as noted)
    Bacon 23.9
    Bacon-egg 24.5
    Bacon-lettuce-tomato, with 1 tbsp. mayonnaise ...27.6
    Barbecued beef, with 1 tbsp. barbecue sauce 24.3
    Barbecued pork, with 1 tbsp. barbecue sauce 24.3
    Bockwurst 23.5
    Bologna, all meat 25.2
    Bologna, with cereal 25.4
    Braunschweiger 24.4

Capicola 23.1
Cervelat, dried 24.1
Cervelat, soft 24.0
Cheese, American 24.1
Cheese, Cheddar 24.3
Cheese, cream (see Sandwiches, cream cheese)
Cheese, Swiss 24.1
Cheese and bacon, grilled 24.9
Chicken, sliced 23.1
Chicken liver, chopped 24.2
Chicken salad, made with 1 tbsp. diced celery and
    1 tbsp. mayonnaise 23.6
Club (bacon-turkey-lettuce-tomato-mayonnaise),
    3-decker 39.1
Corned beef 23.1
Crabmeat, with 1 tbsp. mayonnaise 23.7
Cream cheese 24.2
Cream cheese and jelly 36.9
Egg, fried or scrambled 23.6
Egg, sliced, with 1 tbsp. mayonnaise 23.7
Egg salad, made with 1 tbsp. diced onion and
    1 tbsp. mayonnaise 24.6
Fish cake 33.4
Frankfurter on frankfurter roll, with 2 tsp. mustard 22.9
Ham, baked 23.3
Ham, boiled 23.1
Ham, deviled 23.1
Ham, spiced 23.9
Ham and cheese 23.7

Ham salad, made with 1 tbsp. diced celery and
1 tbsp. mayonnaise 23.6
Hamburger on hamburger roll 21.3
Hamburger on hamburger roll, with cheese 21.7
Hamburger on hamburger roll, with 1 tbsp. catsup 25.0
Headcheese 23.7
Herring, pickled or smoked 23.1
Herring in tomato sauce 25.2
Knockwurst 24.6
Liverwurst, fresh 24.2
Liverwurst, smoked 24.4
Lobster salad, made with 1 tbsp. diced celery and
1 tbsp. mayonnaise 23.8
Meat loaf (luncheon meat) 25.0
Mortadella 23.5
Pate de foie gras 24.5
Peanut butter 28.4
Peanut butter and jelly 41.0
Peanut spread 29.4
Pork sausage 23.1
Roast beef 23.1
Roast pork 23.1
Salami, cooked 23.9
Salami, dried 23.8
Salmon 23.1
Salmon, smoked, with cream cheese 23.6
Salmon salad, made with 1 tbsp. diced celery and
1 tbsp. mayonnaise 23.6
Sardine 23.1

Sardine in mustard or tomato sauce 24.1
Shrimp, fried 28.8
Shrimp paste 23.9
Shrimp salad, made with 1 tbsp. diced celery and
  1 tbsp. mayonnaise 24.5
Steak 23.1
Tomato and lettuce 27.2
Tongue, beef 23.4
Tongue, deviled 23.5
Tuna 23.1
Tuna salad, made with 1 tbsp. diced celery and
  1 tbsp. mayonnaise 23.6
Turkey, sliced 23.1
Turkey salad, made with 1 tbsp. diced celery and
  1 tbsp. mayonnaise 23.6
Vienna sausage 23.3
Sapotes (see Marmalade plums)
Sardines, canned
  Atlantic, in oil, 4 oz. 7
  Pacific, in brine or mustard sauce, with liquid, 4 oz. 1.9
  Pacific, in tomato sauce, with sauce, 4 oz. 1.9
Sauce
  Barbecue, 1 cup 20.0
  Hollandaise, 1 cup 1.4
  Soy, 1 cup 27.6
  Soy, 1 tbsp. 1.7
  Sweet (see Syrup)
  Tartar, 1 cup 9.7
  Tartar, 1 tbsp. 6

White, medium, 1 cup 22.0
White, thin, 1 cup 18.0
Sauerkraut
Canned, 1 lb. 18.1
Canned, with liquid, 1 cup 9.4
Sauerkraut juice, canned, 1 cup 5.6
Sausages
Brown and serve, cooked, 1 lb. 12.7
Brown and serve, cooked, 4 oz. 3.2
Brown and serve, cooked, 1 link
    (3⅞" long × ⅝" diameter) 5
Brown and serve, cooked, 1 patty
    (2⅜" × 1⅞" × ½") 6
Country style 0
Polish, 1 lb. 5.4
Polish, 4 oz. 1.4
Polish, 2.7-oz. sausage (5⅜" long × 1" diameter) .9
Pork, canned, drained, 1 link (3" long × ½"
    diameter) 2
Pork, canned, with liquid, 1 lb. 10.9
Pork, canned, with liquid, 4 oz. (about 7 links) 2.7
Pork, cooked, 1 lb. ....tr.
Pork, cooked, 4 oz. ....tr.
Pork, cooked, 1 link (4" long × ⅞" diameter) ....tr.
Pork, cooked, 1 patty (3⅞" diameter × ¼") .....tr.
Pork and beef, chopped 0
Scrapple, 1 lb. 66.2
Scrapple, 4 oz. 16.4
Souse, 1 lb. 5.4

Souse, 4 oz. 1.4
Vienna, canned, 4 oz. (about 7 sausages) 3
Vienna, canned, 1 sausage (2" long) ....tr.

Scallions (see Onions, green)

Scallops
Bay or sea, fresh, raw, meat only, 4 oz. 3.8
Sea, frozen, breaded, fried, reheated, 4 oz. 12.0

Scrapple, Souse (see Sausages)

Sea bass 0

Sesame seeds
Dried, hulled, 1 cup 26.4
Dried, hulled, 1 tbsp. 1.4

Shad 0

Shad roe 0

Shallots
Peeled, chopped, 1 tbsp. 1.7
Raw, 4 oz. 16.8

Sherbet
Orange, ½ gal. 474.9
Orange, 1 cup 59.4

Shortbread (see Cookies)

Shortening 0

Shrimp
Canned, drained, 1 lb. 3.2
Canned, drained, 10 large shrimp (3¼" long) 4
Canned, drained, 10 medium shrimp (2½" long) .. .2
Canned, drained, 10 small shrimp (2" long) 1
Canned, drained or dry pack, 4 oz. 8
Canned, with liquid, 4 oz. 9

Fresh, breaded, fried, 4 oz. 11.3

Fresh, raw, in shell, 1 lb. 4.7

Fresh, raw, shelled and cleaned, 4 oz. 1.7

Shrimp paste

Canned, 1 oz. 4

Canned, 1 tsp. 1

Smelt 0

Snails, raw, meat only, 4 oz. 2.3

Soft drinks

Club soda 0

Cola, 12 fl. oz. 36.9

Cola, 1 cup 24.8

Cream soda, 12 fl. oz. 40.8

Cream soda, 1 cup 27.2

Fruit flavor (citrus, cherry, grape, etc.), 12 fl. oz. ..44.6

Fruit flavor (citrus, cherry, grape, etc.), 1 cup 29.6

Ginger ale, 12 fl. oz. 29.3

Ginger ale, 1 cup 19.2

Quinine water (tonic), 12 fl. oz. 29.3

Quinine water (tonic), 1 cup 19.2

Root beer, 12 fl. oz. 38.9

Root beer, 1 cup 25.6

Tom Collins mixer, 1 cup 29.6

Sole 0

Sorghum grain, 4 oz. 83.2

Soup, canned, condensed

Asparagus, cream of, diluted with equal part water,

1 cup 10.1

Asparagus, cream of, diluted with equal part whole
milk, 1 cup 16.7
Bean with pork, diluted with equal part water,
1 cup 21.8
Beef broth, bouillon or consomme, diluted with
equal part water, 1 cup 2.6
Beef noodle, diluted with equal part water, 1 cup ..7.0
Celery, cream of, diluted with equal part water,
1 cup 8.9
Celery, cream of, diluted with equal part whole milk,
1 cup 15.2
Chicken, cream of, diluted with equal part water,
1 cup 7.9
Chicken, cream of, diluted with equal part whole milk,
1 cup 14.5
Chicken consomme, diluted with equal part water,
1 cup 1.9
Chicken gumbo, diluted with equal part water,
1 cup 7.4
Chicken noodle, diluted with equal part water,
1 cup 7.9
Chicken vegetable, diluted with equal part water,
1 cup 9.6
Chicken with rice, diluted with equal part water,
1 cup 5.8
Clam chowder, Manhattan style, diluted with equal
part water, 1 cup 12.3
Minestrone, diluted with equal part water, 1 cup ..14.2

Mushroom, cream of, diluted with equal part water,
1 cup 10.1
Mushroom, cream of, diluted with equal part whole
milk, 1 cup 16.2
Onion, diluted with equal part water, 1 cup 5.3
Pea, green, diluted with equal part water, 1 cup ..22.5
Pea, green, diluted with equal part whole milk,
1 cup 29.3
Pea, split, diluted with equal part water, 1 cup ...20.6
Tomato, diluted with equal part water, 1 cup 15.7
Tomato, diluted with equal part whole milk, 1 cup 22.5
Turkey noodle, diluted with equal part water, 1 cup 8.4
Vegetarian vegetable, diluted with equal part water,
1 cup 13.2
Vegetable beef, diluted with equal part water, 1 cup 9.6
Vegetable with beef broth, diluted with equal part
water, 1 cup 13.5
Soup, dehydrated, prepared as noted
Beef noodle (2 oz. mix; 3 cups water), 1 cup 11.5
Chicken noodle (2 oz. mix; 4 cups water), 1 cup ...7.7
Chicken rice (1½ oz. mix; 3 cups water), 1 cup 8.4
Onion (1½ oz. mix; 4 cups water), 1 cup 5.5
Pea, green (4 oz. mix; 3 cups water), 1 cup 20.6
Tomato-vegetable-noodle (2½ oz. mix; 4 cups water),
1 cup 12.2
Sour cream (see Cream)
Soursop
Pureed, 1 cup 36.7
Raw, whole, 1 lb. 50.3

Souse (see Sausages)
Soybean curd (see Bean curd)
Soybean milk, fluid, 4 oz. 2.5
Soybean protein, 4 oz. 17.1
Soybean seeds
    Immature, boiled, drained, 4 oz. 11.5
    Immature, canned, with liquid, 4 oz. 7.2
    Immature, raw, shelled, 1 lb. 59.9
    Mature, dried, cooked, 1 cup 19.4
    Mature, dried, uncooked, 1 cup 70.4
Soybean sprouts, 1 cup 10.8
Soybeans, fermented
    Miso with cereal, 4 oz. 26.7
    Natto, 4 oz. 13.1
Spaghetti
    Canned, in tomato sauce, with cheese, 1 cup 38.5
    Canned, in tomato sauce, with cheese, 1 lb. 69.9
    Canned, in tomato sauce, with cheese, 4 oz. 17.5
    Canned, in tomato sauce, with meatballs, 1 cup ..28.5
    Canned, in tomato sauce, with meatballs, 1 lb. ...51.7
    Canned, in tomato sauce, with meatballs, 4 oz. ...12.9
    Plain, boiled 8–10 minutes, drained, 1 cup 39.1
    Plain, boiled 8–10 minutes, drained, 1 lb. 136.5
    Plain, boiled 14–20 minutes, drained, 1 cup 32.2
    Plain, boiled 14–20 minutes, drained, 1 lb. 104.3
Spareribs 0
Spinach
    Boiled, drained, leaves, 1 cup 6.5
    Boiled, drained, leaves, 1 lb. 16.3

Canned, drained, 1 cup 7.4
Canned, drained, 1 lb. 16.3
Frozen, chopped, boiled, drained, 1 cup 7.6
Frozen, chopped, boiled, drained, 1 lb. 16.8
Frozen, leaves, boiled, drained, 1 cup 7.4
Frozen, leaves, boiled, drained, 1 lb. 17.7
Raw, chopped, 1 cup 2.4
Raw, trimmed, 1 lb. 19.5
Spinach, New Zealand
Boiled, drained, 1 cup 3.8
Boiled, drained, 1 lb. 9.5
Raw, 1 lb. 14.1
Spot 0
Squab 0
Squash, summer
Scallop, boiled, drained, mashed, 1 cup 9.1
Scallop, boiled, drained, sliced, 1 cup 6.8
Scallop, raw, sliced or diced, 1 cup 6.6
Scallop, raw, whole, 1 lb. 22.7
Yellow, boiled, drained, mashed, 1 cup 7.4
Yellow, boiled, drained, sliced, 1 cup 5.6
Yellow, raw, sliced or diced, 1 cup 5.6
Yellow, raw, whole, 1 lb. 19.1
Zucchini, boiled, drained, cubed or diced, 1 cup ...5.3
Zucchini, boiled, drained, mashed, 1 cup 6.0
Zucchini, boiled, drained, sliced, 1 cup 4.5
Zucchini, raw, sliced or diced, 1 cup 4.7
Zucchini, raw, whole, 1 lb. 15.5

Squash, winter
　　Acorn, baked, ½ squash (4″ diameter) 21.8
　　Acorn, baked, mashed, 1 cup 28.7
　　Acorn, boiled, mashed, 1 cup 20.6
　　Acorn, raw, whole, 1 lb. 38.6
　　Acorn, raw, whole, 1 squash (4″ diameter) 48.3
　　Butternut, baked, mashed, 1 cup 35.9
　　Butternut, boiled, mashed, 1 cup 25.5
　　Butternut, raw, whole, 1 lb. 44.4
　　Hubbard, baked, mashed, 1 cup 24.0
　　Hubbard, boiled, mashed, 1 cup 16.9
　　Hubbard, raw, whole, 1 lb. 28.1
　　Frozen, cooked, 1 cup 22.1
　　Frozen, cooked, 1 lb. 41.7
Squash seed kernels, dried, 1 cup 21.0
Starch (see Cornstarch)
Strawberries
　　Canned, water pack, with liquid, 1 cup 13.6
　　Canned, water pack, with liquid, 1 lb. 25.4
　　Fresh, whole, 1 cup 12.5
　　Fresh, whole, capped, trimmed, 1 lb. 38.1
　　Frozen, sweetened, sliced, 1 cup 70.9
　　Frozen, sweetened, sliced, 1 lb. 126.1
　　Frozen, sweetened, whole, 1 cup 59.9
　　Frozen, sweetened, whole, 1 lb. 106.6
Sturgeon, fresh or smoked 0
Succotash
　　Frozen, boiled, drained, 1 cup 34.9
　　Frozen, boiled, drained, 1 lb. 93.0

Sugar

    Beet or cane, brown, firmly packed, 1 cup 212.1

    Beet or cane, brown, loosely packed, 1 cup 139.8

    Beet or cane, granulated, 1 cup 199.0

    Beet or cane, granulated, 1 tbsp. 11.9

    Beet or cane, granulated, 1 tsp. 4.0

    Beet or cane, granulated, 1 lump

      ($1\frac{1}{8}'' \times \frac{3}{4}'' \times \frac{5}{16}''$) 5.0

    Beet or cane, powdered, sifted, 1 cup 99.5

    Beet or cane, powdered, unsifted, 1 cup 119.4

    Beet or cane, powdered, unsifted, 1 tbsp. 8.0

    Maple, 1-oz. piece 25.5

Sunflower seed kernels

    Hulled, 1 cup 28.9

    Hulled, 1 lb. 90.3

    In hull, 1 cup 9.1

    In hull, 1 lb. 48.7

    In hull, 4 oz. 12.2

Surinam cherry (see Pitanga)

Sweet potatoes (see Potatoes, sweet)

Sweetbreads, all kinds 0

Swordfish 0

Syrup

    Chocolate, fudge type, 1 cup 162.0

    Chocolate, fudge type, 1 tbsp. 10.0

    Chocolate, thin type, 1 cup 188.1

    Chocolate, thin type, 1 tbsp. 11.8

    Corn, light or dark, 1 cup 246.0

    Corn, light or dark, 1 tbsp. 15.4

Maple, 1 cup 204.8
Maple, 1 tbsp. 12.8
Molasses, blackstrap, 1 cup 180.4
Molasses, blackstrap, 1 tbsp. 11.0
Molasses, light, 1 cup 213.2
Molasses, light, 1 tbsp. 13.0
Molasses, medium, 1 cup 196.8
Molasses, medium, 1 tbsp. 12.0
Sorghum, 1 cup 224.4
Sorghum, 1 tbsp. 14.0
Table blend (cane and maple), 1 cup 204.8
Table blend (cane and maple), 1 tbsp. 12.8
Table blend (chiefly light and dark corn), 1 cup..246.0
Table blend (chiefly light and dark corn), 1 tbsp. ..15.4

T

Tamarind

    Fresh, shelled and seeded, 4 oz. 71.3

    Whole, 1 lb. 136.1

Tangelo juice, fresh, 1 cup 24.0

Tangelos, used for juices

    1 large tangelo (2¾" diameter) 11.1

    1 small tangelo (2¼" diameter) 6.6

Tangerine juice

    Canned, sweetened, 1 cup 29.9

    Frozen, unsweetened, diluted, 1 cup 26.8

    Fresh or canned, unsweetened, 1 cup 24.9

    Fresh or canned, unsweetened, 1 fl. oz. 3.2

Tangerines

    Fresh, sections, 1 cup 22.6

    Fresh, whole, 1 lb. 38.9

    Fresh, whole, 1 average tangerine (2⅜" diameter) 10.0

    Fresh whole, 1 large tangerine (2½" diameter) ..11.7

Tapioca

    Dried, 1 cup 131.3

Dried, 1 tbsp. 7.3
Taro
    Raw, corms and tubers, 1 lb. 90.3
    Raw, leaves and stems, 1 lb. 33.6
Tartar sauce (see Sauce)
Tea, instant, dry form, 1 tsp. 4
Thuringer
    1 lb. 7.3
    4 oz. 1.8
Tilefish 0
Tomato catsup (see Catsup)
Tomato juice
    Canned or bottled, 1 cup 10.4
    Canned or bottled, 1 fl. oz. 1.3
Tomato juice cocktail
    Canned or bottled, 1 cup 12.2
    Canned or bottled, 1 fl. oz. 1.5
Tomato paste
    Canned, 1 cup 48.7
    Canned, 6-oz. can 31.6
Tomato puree
    Canned, 1 lb. 40.4
    Canned, 4 oz. 10.1
Tomatoes
    Green, whole, 1 lb. 21.1
    Ripe, boiled, 1 cup 13.3
    Ripe, canned, with liquid, 1 cup 10.4
    Ripe, canned, with liquid, 1 lb. 19.5

Ripe, raw, whole, 1 lb. 21.3

Ripe, raw, whole, 1 large tomato (3″ diameter) ...8.6

Ripe, raw, whole, 1 small tomato (2⅖″ diameter) ..4.3

Ripe, raw, whole, peeled, 1 large tomato
  (3″ diameter) 8.3

Ripe, raw, whole, peeled, 1 small tomato
  (2⅖″ diameter) 4.1

Tongue

Beef, medium-fat, braised, 4 oz. 5

Calf, braised, 4 oz. 1.1

Canned or pickled, 4 oz. 3

Hog or lamb, braised, 4 oz. 6

Potted or deviled, 4 oz. 8

Sheep, braised, 4 oz. 2.7

Tripe 0

Trout 0

Tuna, fresh or canned 0

Turbot 0

Turkey, fresh or canned 0

Turkey giblets, simmered, chopped or diced, 1 cup 2.3

Turkey gizzards, simmered, chopped or diced, 1 cup 1.6

Turkey pot pie, frozen, 8-oz. pie 45.6

Turnip greens

Canned, with liquid, 1 cup 7.4

Fresh, boiled, drained, 1 cup 5.0

Fresh, raw, whole, 1 lb. 19.0

Frozen, chopped, boiled, drained, 1 cup 6.4

Turnips

Boiled, drained, cubed, 1 cup 7.6

Boiled, drained, mashed, 1 cup 11.3
Fresh, raw, cubed or sliced, 1 cup 8.6
Fresh, raw, without tops, untrimmed, 1 lb. 25.7

	grams
Veal	0
Vegetable juice cocktail	
Canned or bottled, 1 cup	8.7
Canned or bottled, 1 fl. oz.	1.1
Vegetables (see individual listings)	
Vegetables, mixed	
Frozen, boiled, drained, 1 cup	24.4
Frozen, boiled, drained, 1 lb.	60.8
Venison	0
Vienna sausage (see Sausages)	
Vinegar	
Cider, 1 tbsp.	.9
Distilled, 1 tbsp.	.8
Vine spinach, raw, 4 oz.	3.9
Vodka (see Alcoholic Beverages, pages 130–32)	

grams

Waffles
    Frozen, prebaked, 1 waffle (4⅝″ × 3¾″) 14.3
    Mix, made with egg and milk, 1 round
       (7″ diameter) 27.2
    Mix, made with egg and milk, 1 square (9″ × 9″) 72.4
    Mix, made with egg and milk, 1 square
       (4½″ × 4½″) 18.1

Walnuts
    Black, in shell, 1 lb. 14.8
    Black, in shell, 4 oz. 3.7
    Black, shelled, 1 lb. 67.1
    Black, shelled, 4 oz. 16.8
    Black, shelled, chopped, 1 cup 18.5
    Black, shelled, chopped, 1 tbsp. 1.2
    English, 10 large nuts 7.8
    English, in shell, 1 lb. 32.2
    English, in shell, 4 oz. 8.1
    English, shelled, 1 lb. 71.7
    English, shelled, 4 oz. 18.0

English, chopped, 1 cup 19.0
English, chopped, 1 tbsp. 1.3
English, halves, 1 cup 15.8
Water chestnuts, raw
    Peeled, 4 oz. 21.7
    Whole, 1 lb. 66.4
    Whole, 5–7 corms (4 oz.) 16.6
Watercress
    Chopped, 1 cup 3.8
    Whole, with stems, 1 cup 1.1
    Whole, with stems, 1 lb. 12.5
Watermelon
    Diced, 1 cup 10.2
    Whole, with rind, 1 lb. 13.4
    With rind, 1 wedge (4" × 8") 27.3
Weakfish 0
West Indian cherry (see Acerola)
Wheat
    Parboiled (see Bulgur)
    Whole grain, durum, 4 oz. 79.5
    Whole grain, hard red, 4 oz. 78.4
    Whole grain, soft red, 4 oz. 81.7
    Whole grain, white, 4 oz. 85.5
Wheat bran, commercially milled, 4 oz. 70.2
Wheat cereal (see Cereal)
Wheat germ, toasted, 1 tbsp. 3.0
Whey, fluid, 1 cup 12.5
Whiskey (see Alcoholic Beverages, pages 130–32)
White sauce (see Sauce)

Whitefish, fresh or smoked 0
Wild rice
    Raw, 1 cup 120.5
    Raw, 4 oz. 85.4
Wine (see Alcoholic Beverages, pages 130–32)

Y

grams

Yams
    Candied (see Potatoes, sweet)
    Tuber, raw, whole, with skin, 1 lb. 90.5
Yeast, baker's
    Compressed, 1 cake (about ¾ oz.) 2.3
    Dry, active, 1 pkg. (¼ oz.) or tbsp. 2.7
Yogurt, plain
    Made from partially skim milk, 1 cup 12.7
    Made from partially skim milk, 8-oz. container ...11.8
    Made from whole milk, 1 cup 12.0
    Made from whole milk, 8-oz. container 11.1

Z

grams

Zucchini (see Squash, summer)
Zwieback (see Crackers)

ALCOHOLIC BEVERAGES

grams

Beer
    Domestic, 4.5% alcohol, 8 fl. oz. 9.1
    Domestic, 4.5% alcohol, 12-fl. oz. can or bottle. . .13.7
Distilled spirits (brandy, gin, rum, rye, Scotch,
    vodka, whiskey, etc.), 3 fl. oz. . . . . .tr.
Liqueurs and flavored spirits: *
    Anise liqueur, 1 fl. oz. 1.0
    Anisette liqueur, 1 fl. oz. 10.5
    Apricot liqueur, 1 fl. oz. .8.5
    B & B, 1 fl. oz. 5.7
    Benedictine, 1 fl. oz. 10.3
    Blackberry liqueur, 1 fl. oz. 8.0
    Brandy, flavored:
        Apricot, 1 fl. oz. 7.5
        Blackberry, 1 fl. oz. .8.0
        Cherry, 1 fl. oz. 8.0
        Ginger, 1 fl. oz. 4.5
        Peach, 1 fl. oz. 8.0
    Cherry liqueur, 1 fl. oz. .9.0
    Coffee liqueur (Tia Maria), 1 fl. oz. 10.0
    Creme d'almond liqueur, 1 fl. oz. 14.0
    Creme de cacao liqueur, 1 fl. oz. 13.5
    Creme de cassis liqueur, 1 fl. oz. 14.5
    Creme de menthe liqueur, 1 fl. oz. 13.5
    Curacao liqueur, 1 fl. oz. 10.0
    Drambuie, 1 fl. oz. 11.0
    Kummel liqueur, 1 fl. oz. 5.0

Maraschino cherry liqueur, 1 fl. oz. 10.4
Peach liqueur, 1 fl. oz. 9.1
Peppermint schnapps, 1 fl. oz. 8.4
Rock and rye liqueur, 1 fl. oz. 7.6
Sloe gin, 1 fl. oz. 6.2
Southern Comfort, 1 fl. oz. 3.5
Triple Sec, 1 fl. oz. 9.7
Vodka, flavored, 1 fl. oz. .8.0
Wines: *
Asti Spumante, 4 fl. oz. .24.0
Bordeaux, burgundy (see Dinner wine, below)
Burgundy, sparkling, 4 fl. oz. 3.3
Catawba, 4 fl. oz. 13.0
Chablis (see Dinner wine, below)
Champagne, dry, domestic, 4 fl. oz. 1.7
Champagne, pink, domestic, 4 fl. oz. 3.5
Cherry Kijafa, 4 fl. oz. 20.4
Claret, Chianti (see Dinner wine, below)
Cold Duck (Italian Swiss Colony Gold Medal),
    4 fl. oz. 5.7
Dinner (table) wine, dry, 12.2% alcohol, 4 fl. oz. . .4.8
Kosher, medium (Manischewitz), 4 fl. oz. 5.7
Kosher, sweet (Manischewitz), 4 fl. oz. 20.5
Madeira, 4 fl. oz. 12.6
Muscatel, 4 fl. oz. 12.6
Port, ruby, 4 fl. oz. 13.2
Port, tawny, 4 fl. oz. 13.0

*Unless a brand name is specified, figures that are listed for
liqueurs and wines are based on an average of several brands.

Sauterne (dessert wine), 4 fl. oz. 10.6
Sherry, 4 fl. oz. 6.0
Sherry, cream, 4 fl. oz. 12.3
Vermouth, dry, 4 fl. oz. 3.1
Vermouth, sweet, 4 fl. oz. 15.9

LOW-GRAM SNACKS & TIDBITS

	grams
Almonds, 10 nuts	2.0
Anchovies, 2-oz. can	.1
Bacon, fried, 2 medium slices	.5
Bacon, Canadian, fried, 2 slices	.2
Beef, roast	0
Blood sausage, 2 oz.	.2
Bockwurst, 2 oz.	.4
Bologna, all meat, 2 oz.	2.1
Bouillon, 1 cup (made with 1 bouillon cube)	.2
Braunschweiger, 2 oz.	1.3
Brazil nuts, 3 large nuts	1.5
Capicola	0
Caviar, 1 oz.	.9
Cervelat, 2 oz.	.9
Cheese	
American or pimiento, 1 oz.	.5
Blue or Roquefort, 1 oz.	.6
Brick, 1 oz.	.5
Camembert, 1 oz.	.5
Cheddar, domestic, 1 oz.	.6
Cream, 1 tbsp.	.3
Limburger, 1 oz.	.6
Swiss, 1 oz.	.5
Chicken, canned or roast	0
Clams, canned, drained, 4 oz.	2.2
Crabmeat cocktail (½ cup meat and 1 tbsp. mayonnaise)	.7
Eel, smoked	0

Eggs, hard-boiled, 1 medium egg 4

Filberts or hazelnuts, 10 nuts 2.3

Fish 0

Frankfurters, 1 average frankfurter 1.1

Gum, chewing, candy-coated, 1 piece 1.6

Ham, boiled, or deviled 0

Ham, spiced, 4 oz. 1.6

Headcheese, 2 oz. 6

Herring, kippered, pickled or smoked 0

Hickory nuts, in shell, 2 oz. 2.6

Knockwurst, 1 average link 1.5

Liver, chicken, chopped, ½ cup 2.2

Liverwurst, fresh, 2 oz. 1.1

Lobster cocktail (½ cup meat and 1 tbsp. mayonnaise).. .5

Lobster paste, 1 oz. 4

Meat loaf (luncheon meat), 2 oz. 1.9

Mortadella, 2 oz. 4

Mussels, canned, 4 oz. 1.7

Olives, green, 10 large olives 5

Olives, ripe, 10 large olives 1.2

Oysters, Eastern, 2 medium or 3 small oysters 1.0

Pate de foie gras, 1 tbsp. 6

Peanuts, 10 jumbo peanuts 3.7

Pickles, dill, ½ large pickle 1.5

Pickles, sour, ½ large pickle 1.4

Pig's feet 0

Polish sausage, 2.7-oz. sausage 9

Popcorn, plain, 1 cup 4.6

Pork, roast 0

Pork sausage, 4 oz. ....tr.

Pretzel sticks, 10 sticks (2¼" long) 2.3

Salami, cooked, 2 oz. 8

Salami, dry, 2 oz. 7

Salmon, canned, fresh or smoked 0

Salmon salad, 1 cup (made with 2 tbsp. diced celery
  and 2 tbsp. mayonnaise) 1.2

Sardines, canned in oil, 4 oz. 7

Sardines, canned in mustard or tomato sauce, 4 oz. 1.9

Shrimp, canned, 10 large shrimp 4

Shrimp paste, 1 oz. 4

Tongue, canned or pickled, 4 oz. 3

Tuna, canned 0

Tuna salad, 1 cup (made with 2 tbsp. diced celery
  and 2 tbsp. mayonnaise) 1.2

Vienna sausage, 4 oz. (about 7 sausages) 3

Walnuts, English, 5 large nuts 3.9

TWO WEEKS OF
LOW-GRAM
MENUS

As noted earlier, limiting your intake of carbohydrates to 60 (or less) grams a day will result in your losing weight. On the pages that follow are two weeks of low-gram menus to start you on your weight-loss program. The fourteen menus are typical low-carbohydrate meals—tempting and tantalizing yet still within the 60 grams a day that you're allowed on this dream of a diet!

Bear in mind, however, that these menus are merely suggestions. You are, of course, free to make any substitutions you wish. Just be sure that you are accurate about substitutions—and, especially if you're planning to stay on this diet for longer than two weeks, pick foods that have the same, or similar, nutritional value. For example, if you can't bear green beans, replace them with another vegetable—not with a cookie or a piece of gum. (Substituting a cookie may not prevent you from losing weight, but if you ignore sound nutrition, you may pay for it with your health!)

You'll notice as you glance through the menus that some foods are listed by specific amounts and/or weights (for example, "2 frankfurters" or "2 tbsp. sour cream" or "1 cup cabbage") and other foods are listed only by name (for example, "sirloin steak" or "chicken" or "lamb chops"). The difference in the two kinds of listings is simple: When a specific amount is called for, it means that the dedicated dieter should eat **exactly** that amount—and no more! When no amount is specified, it means that the dieter may eat **as much of the food** as he or she wishes, since that food contains 0 carbohydrate grams. That's the beauty of the low-carbohydrate diet. You don't ever have to feign contentment or pretend fulfillment. Still hungry after you've eaten everything on the menu? Don't hold back. Have another hamburger or a chicken leg or a third, fourth, or even a fifth lamb chop! Chances are, you won't be hungry on this diet, but if you are, there's no need to stay hungry, no need to suffer, no need to get tense and irritable. Try it. You'll see. You have nothing to lose but those extra pounds.

DAY 1

BREAKFAST   grams
2 medium eggs, fried 8
    in 2 tbsp. butter or margarine 2
4 pork sausage links, fried .... tr.
1 thin slice white bread, toasted 8.8
    spread with 1 tbsp. cream cheese 3
Coffee with 1 tbsp. heavy cream 5

                                              —————
                                             10.6

LUNCH
1 cup chicken gumbo soup 7.4
Lake or brook trout, broiled 0
    with 2 tbsp. butter or margarine 2
    and 1 tbsp. lemon juice 1.2
⅔ cup shredded raw cabbage 3.3
    mixed with 2 tbsp. mayonnaise 6
½ cup fresh red raspberries 8.4

                                              —————
                                             21.1

DINNER
1½ oz. liquor (with water, soda, or on the rocks) .... tr.
Sirloin steak, broiled 0
    with 2 tbsp. garlic butter 4
½ cup mashed (with butter and milk) potatoes 12.9
½ head Boston lettuce, shredded 2.1

```
    and ⅓ tomato, sliced ........................ 2.7
    with 2 tbsp. Italian dressing ................. 2.0
1 oz. Camembert cheese ......................... .5
1 rye wafer ...................................... 5.0
                                                 ─────
                                                  25.6
```

Total for the Day: 57.3

DAY 2

BREAKFAST grams

2 medium eggs, scrambled 8
   with smoked salmon, diced 0
   and 1 tbsp. chopped onion 9
   in 2 tbsp. butter or margarine 2
1 small slice Italian bread 5.6
   spread with 1 tbsp. cream cheese 3
Coffee with 1 tbsp. heavy cream 5

8.3

LUNCH

1 cup chicken consomme 1.9
Ground beef patty, broiled 0
   with 1 oz. Cheddar cheese 6
   atop ½ hamburger roll 10.6
   spread with 1 tsp. catsup 1.3
½ large dill pickle 1.5
1 cup coleslaw (made with mayonnaise) 5.8
½ cup whole milk 6.0

27.7

DINNER

1 gin or vodka martini 3
½ tomato 4.3
   stuffed with ½ cup canned crabmeat 8

```
         topped with 1 tbsp. mayonnaise ............... .3
Chicken breasts, sauteed ......................... 0
    in 3 tbsp. tarragon butter ..................... .3
½ cup fresh green beans, boiled .................. 3.4
    topped with 1 tbsp. butter or margarine ......... .1
    and 1 tbsp. chopped almonds ................. 1.6
¾ cup fresh strawberries ......................... 9.4
    with 2 tbsp. heavy cream ..................... 1.0
                                                  ——
                                                  21.5
```

Total for the Day: 57.5

DAY 3

BREAKFAST grams

2-egg (medium) omelet	.8
filled with diced boiled ham	0
and 1 oz. Swiss cheese	.5
cooked in 2 tbsp. butter or margarine	.2
½ cloverleaf roll	7.4
spread with 1 tbsp. cream cheese	.3
Coffee with 1 tbsp. heavy cream	.5
	9.7

LUNCH

1 cup beef broth	2.6
Tuna fish	0
mixed with ¼ cup chopped celery	1.2
and 2 tbsp. mayonnaise	.6
atop 2 iceberg lettuce leaves	1.2
½ tomato, sliced	4.3
2 green onions	3.2
1 zwieback toast	5.2
1 oz. Cheddar cheese	.6
	18.9

DINNER

3 oz. dry wine	3.6

London broil slices, broiled 0
   with ½ cup fresh sliced mushrooms 1.6
   and 2 tbsp. butter or margarine 2
8 fresh asparagus spears, steamed 4.4
   topped with 2 tbsp. melted butter 2
   and 1 tbsp. lemon juice 1.2
½ baked potato 16.4
   topped with 1 tbsp. sour cream 7

——————
28.3

Total for the Day: 56.9

DAY 4

BREAKFAST grams

½ cup tomato juice 5.2
Kippered herring, sauteed 0
    with ¼ onion, sliced 2.4
    in 2 tbsp. butter or margarine 2
3 saltines 6.0
1 oz. American cheese 5
Coffee with 1 tbsp. heavy cream 5

                             —
                           14.8

LUNCH

10 large canned shrimp, chilled 4
    topped with 1 tbsp. chili sauce 3.7
Chicken, broiled 0
    brushed with 2 tbsp. garlic butter 4
1 cup chilled California avocado cubes 9.0
    mixed with 1 tbsp. olive oil 0
    and 1 tbsp. lemon juice 1.2
1 medium peach 9.7

                             —
                           24.4

DINNER

1½ oz. liquor (with water, soda, or on the rocks) .... tr.
Salmon steak, broiled 0
    with 2 tbsp. dill butter 2

½ tomato, broiled 4.3
    with 1 tbsp. grated Parmesan cheese 2
¼ head iceberg lettuce, shredded 3.9
    and ½ small green pepper, sliced 1.8
    topped with 1 tbsp. French dressing 2.8
1 small slice Italian bread 5.6
    spread with 1 tbsp. butter 1
                                     ——
                                     18.9

Total for the Day: 58.1

DAY 5

BREAKFAST grams
½ cup fresh grapefruit sections 10.1
2 medium eggs, soft-boiled 8
4 oz. baked cured ham 3
1 saltine 2.0
    spread with 1 tbsp. butter 1
Coffee with 1 tbsp. heavy cream 5

                                      13.8

LUNCH
¾ cup onion soup 4.1
    topped with 1 oz. melted Swiss cheese 5
1 cup raw chopped spinach 2.4
    mixed with ¼ cup raw sliced mushrooms 8
    and 4 slices fried bacon, crumbled 1.0
    and 1 medium hard-boiled egg, chopped 4
    topped with 2 tbsp. Italian dressing 2.0
3 oz. dry wine 3.6
¼ cantaloupe melon 10.2

                                        25.0

DINNER
1½ oz. liquor (with water, soda, or on the rocks) .... tr.
Fillet of sole, broiled 0
    basted with 2 tbsp. butter 2

and 1 oz. dry white wine 1.2
1 cup frozen broccoli spears, boiled 7.0
    topped with 1 tbsp. melted butter 1
1 head French endive, shredded 1.7
    topped with 1 tbsp. blue cheese dressing 1.1
2 fresh apricots 9.2

                                                  20.5

Total for the Day: 59.3

BREAKFAST   grams

½ cup puffed wheat (unsweetened) 5.9

    with 4 tbsp. light cream 2.4

    and 1 tsp. sugar 4.0

2-egg (medium) omelet 8

    filled with 1 oz. American cheese 5

    cooked in 2 tbsp. butter or margarine 2

4 slices Canadian bacon, fried 4

Coffee with 1 tbsp. heavy cream 5

                                        ——

                                     14.7

LUNCH

1 cup chicken consomme 1.9

3 frankfurters, broiled or fried 3.3

3 tsp. mustard 9

½ cup canned sauerkraut 4.7

½ large dill pickle 1.5

1 small slice Italian bread 5.6

    spread with 1 tbsp. butter 1

1 medium fresh peach 9.7

                                        ——

                                     27.7

DINNER

1 gin or vodka martini 3

Smoked salmon slices 0
    with lemon wedge (⅙ of lemon) 1.0
Lamb chops, broiled 0
1 cup raw sliced mushrooms, sauteed 3.1
    with 2 tbsp. chopped almonds 3.2
    in 2 tbsp. butter or margarine 2
1 cup shredded romaine lettuce 1.9
    with 6–7 large cucumber slices 9
    and 2 green onions, diced 3.2
    topped with 1 tbsp. Russian dressing 1.6
Coffee with 1 tbsp. heavy cream 5
1 oz. brandy .... tr.
                                       ——

                                    15.9

Total for the Day: 58.3

BREAKFAST grams

½ cup fresh strawberries 6.3

   topped with 2 tbsp. sour cream 1.0

2 medium eggs, scrambled 8

   with 2 oz. salami, diced 7

   and ¼ cup chopped green pepper 1.8

   in 2 tbsp. butter or margarine 2

Coffee with 1 tbsp. heavy cream 5

————

11.3

LUNCH

Antipasto (sardines, boiled ham, 1 oz. Swiss cheese,
   1 oz. canned pimiento, 5 anchovies, 4 large green
   olives, 2 iceberg lettuce leaves, with 2 tbsp.
   vinegar and olive oil) 4.7

4 oz. chicken livers, simmered 3.5

   with 4 slices bacon 1.0

   and 1 tbsp. chopped onion 9

   atop 1 thin slice white bread, toasted 8.8

½ glass whole milk 6.0

————

24.9

DINNER

3 oz. dry wine 3.6

1 oz. pate de foie gras 1.4

with 1 rye wafer 5.0
spread with 1 tbsp. butter 1
Prime ribs of beef, roasted 0
1 tbsp. prepared horseradish 1.4
1 cup sliced zucchini, boiled 4.5
½ head Boston lettuce, shredded 2.1
and ½ tomato, sliced 4.3
topped with 2 tbsp. vinegar-oil (equal parts) 9

_____

23.3

Total for the Day: 59.5

DAY 8

BREAKFAST grams

⅔ cup corn flakes 14.2

    with 3 tbsp. fresh red raspberries 3.2

    and ¼ cup heavy cream 1.9

2 medium eggs, baked 8

    with 1 tbsp. butter or margarine 1

3 pork sausage patties, fried .... tr.

Coffee with 1 tbsp. heavy cream 5

                                       ————

                                       20.7

LUNCH

Wine spritzer (3 oz. dry wine and soda) 3.6

8 oz. lobster meat, steamed 8

    served with ¼ cup melted butter 3

1 cup raw shredded cabbage 4.9

    mixed with 1 tbsp. raisins 7.0

    and 2 tbsp. mayonnaise 6

    and ½ tbsp. lemon juice 6

1 oz. Camembert cheese 5

                                         ————

                                       18.3

DINNER

1½ oz. liquor (with water, soda, or on the rocks) .... tr.

Veal cutlets, sauteed 0

    in 3 tbsp. butter 3

and ¼ cup dry vermouth 1.6
½ cup cauliflower buds, boiled 2.6
1 cup frozen collard greens, sauteed 9.5
with ½ clove garlic and olive oil 5
Coffee with 1 tbsp. heavy cream 5

———
15.0

Total for the Day: 54.0

BREAKFAST

	grams
⅔ cup tomato juice	7.0
Smoked salmon slices	0
Smoked whitefish chunks	0
Smoked sturgeon slices	0
½ thin slice white bread	4.4
spread with 1 tbsp. cream cheese	.3
Coffee with 1 tbsp. heavy cream	.5

12.2

LUNCH

1 Rob Roy (with dry vermouth)	1.0
Roast Chicken	0
1 corn on the cob, boiled	16.2
spread with 1 tbsp. butter	.1
½ cup fresh spinach, boiled	3.3
mixed with 1 tbsp. heated butter	.1
and 1 tbsp. heated heavy cream	.5
½ cup whole milk	6.0

27.2

DINNER

3 oz. dry wine	3.6
Pork spareribs, broiled	0
brushed with ¼ cup tomato juice	2.6

mixed with 2 tbsp. soy sauce 3.4
¾ cup shredded red cabbage, sauteed 4.7
in 2 tbsp. bacon fat .... tr.
¾ cup zucchini, boiled 3.4
with ¼ peeled tomato 2.1

———

19.8

Total for the Day: 59.2

BREAKFAST

		grams
3 medium eggs, scrambled	....	1.2
in 2 tbsp. butter or margarine	....	.2
6 pork sausage links, fried	....	tr.
1 thin slice white bread, toasted	....	8.8
1 oz. Cheddar cheese	....	.6
1 oz. Swiss cheese	....	.5
½ cup whole milk	....	6.0

                                                    17.3

LUNCH

3 oz. dry wine	....	3.6
Salad Nicoise (tuna fish, 5 ripe olives, ½ tomato, ¼ cup sliced onions, 1 medium hard-boiled egg, ¼ cup raw green pepper slices)	....	8.2
atop 2 cups shredded romaine lettuce	....	3.8
with ¼ cup vinegar-oil (equal parts)	....	1.8
½ cup fresh peach slices	....	8.3
flavored with 1 tbsp. brandy	....	tr.

                                                    25.7

DINNER

1 gin or vodka martini	....	.3
2 large celery stalks	....	3.2
stuffed with 1 oz. Roquefort cheese	....	.6

mixed with 1 oz. cream cheese 6
Roast leg of lamb 0
8 fresh asparagus stalks, steamed 4.4
    topped with ¼ cup Hollandaise sauce 4
½ cup cooked fresh carrots, diced 5.2
Coffee with 1 tbsp. heavy cream 5

—————

15.2

Total for the Day: 58.2

DAY 11

BREAKFAST   grams

½ cup vegetable juice 4.4

2 medium eggs, fried 8

    in 2 tbsp. butter or margarine 2

4 slices bacon, fried 1.0

2 saltines 4.0

    spread with 2 tsp. cream cheese 2

Coffee with 1 tbsp. heavy cream 5

                                             11.1

LUNCH

1 cup turkey noodle soup 8.4

Cold roast beef, turkey, boiled ham slices 0

1 cup shredded iceberg lettuce 1.6

    mixed with ½ cup chopped watercress 1.9

    and ¼ cup sliced raw mushrooms 8

    and 2 tbsp. Italian dressing 2.0

½ cup fresh blueberries 11.1

    topped with 3 tbsp. whipped cream 7

                                             26.5

DINNER

1½ oz. liquor (with water, soda, or on the rocks) .... tr.

Roast loin of pork 0

1 cup fresh Brussels sprouts, sauteed 9.9
    in olive oil and ¼ garlic clove 3
½ tomato, broiled 4.3
    with 1 tbsp. grated Parmesan cheese 2
2 vanilla wafers 6.0
Coffee with 1 tbsp. heavy cream 5
                                     —
                                 21.2

Total for the Day: 58.8

DAY 12

BREAKFAST grams

⅔ cup diced cantaloupe 8.0

    with 2 tbsp. creamed cottage cheese 8

Smelts, fried 0

    in 2 tbsp. butter or margarine 2

½ cup whole milk 6.0

                                               ⎯⎯⎯

                                               15.0

LUNCH

1½ oz. liquor (with water, soda, or on the rocks) .... tr.

Halibut or swordfish steak, broiled 0

    with 2 tbsp. butter or margarine 2

    and 1 tbsp. lemon juice 1.2

½ baked potato 16.4

    topped with 1 tbsp. sour cream 5

    mixed with ½ tbsp. chopped chives 1

1 cup shredded romaine lettuce 1.9

    mixed with ½ cup California avocado cubes 4.5

    and 2 tbsp. vinegar-oil (equal parts) 9

Coffee with 1 tbsp. heavy cream 5

                                               ⎯⎯⎯

                                               26.2

DINNER

1 cup onion soup 5.3

    with 2 tbsp. shredded Parmesan cheese 4

3 medium eggs, poached 1.2

    over 6 slices fried Canadian bacon 6

    topped with ½ cup Hollandaise sauce 7

1 thin slice white bread, toasted 8.8

    spread with 1 tbsp. butter 1

1 oz. Camembert cheese 5

                                      17.6

Total for the Day: 58.8

DAY 13

BREAKFAST   grams
⅓ Florida orange 5.6
2 medium eggs, scrambled 8
   with boiled ham, diced 0
   and 1 oz. Cheddar cheese 6
   in 2 tbsp. butter or margarine 2
4 pork sausage patties .... tr.
Coffee with 1 tbsp. heavy cream 5
                                               —
                                              7.7

LUNCH
½ California avocado 6.5
   filled with diced chicken meat 0
   mixed with ¼ cup diced celery 1.2
   and 2 tbsp. mayonnaise 6
Roast duckling 0
½ cup peeled apple quarters, sauteed 8.8
   in 1 tbsp. butter 1
¾ cup boiled turnips, cubed 5.7
   mashed with 2 tbsp. butter 2
   and 2 tbsp. heavy cream 1.0
Espresso with cognac .... tr.
                                               —
                                            24.1

DINNER

3 oz. dry wine 3.6
Chicken or veal cutlets, thinly sliced 0
     topped with 6 tbsp. pureed tomatoes 7.5
     and 3 tbsp. grated Parmesan cheese 6
⅓ cup cooked (14–20 minutes) spaghetti 10.7
     mixed with garlic (½ clove) and olive oil 5
     and 1 tbsp. chopped parsley 3
1 cup shredded iceberg lettuce 1.6
     mixed with ½ cup whole watercress 6
     and 2 fried bacon slices, crumbled 5
     topped with 2 tbsp. Italian dressing 2.0

                                             ——
                                        27.9

Total for the Day: 59.7

BREAKFAST grams

2 medium eggs, fried	.8
in 2 tbsp. butter or margarine	.2
4 slices fried bacon	1.0
4 pork sausage links	tr.
Boiled ham slices	0
½ thin slice white bread	4.4
spread with 2 tsp. cream cheese	.2
½ cup whole milk	6.0
	12.6

LUNCH

1 gin or vodka martini	.3
2 saltines	4.0
spread with 1 tbsp. sour cream	.5
and topped with 1 tbsp. caviar	.5
T-bone or porterhouse steak	0
4 oz. canned potatoes, sauteed	11.2
with 1 tbsp. chopped onion	.9
and 2 tbsp. chopped green pepper	.5
in 2 tbsp. butter or margarine	.2
1 cup boiled fresh broccoli	7.0
topped with ¼ cup Hollandaise sauce	.4
Coffee with 1 tbsp. heavy cream	.5
	26.0

DINNER

3 oz. dry wine	3.6
4 oz. scallops, sauteed	3.8
in garlic (½ clove) and 3 tbsp. butter	.8
Roast turkey	0
with ¼ cup chopped fresh cranberries	3.0
¾ cup canned green beans, chilled	5.3
mixed with 1 tbsp. chopped onions	.9
and 2 tbsp. Italian dressing	2.0
1 oz. Cheddar cheese	.6
	20.0

Total for the Day: 58.6

TOTAL YOUR GRAMS

DAY 1:

breakfast ....

lunch ....

dinner ....

snacks ....

daily total:

DAY 2:

breakfast ....

lunch ....

dinner ....

snacks ....

daily total:

DAY 3:

breakfast ....

lunch ....

dinner ....

snacks ....

daily total:

DAY 4:

breakfast ....

lunch ....

dinner ....

snacks ....

daily total:

DAY 5:

breakfast ....

lunch ....

dinner ....

snacks ....

daily total:

DAY 6:

breakfast ....

lunch ....

dinner ....

snacks ....

daily total:

DAY 7:

breakfast ....

lunch ....

dinner ....

snacks ....

daily total:

DAY 8:

breakfast ....

lunch ....

dinner ....

snacks ....

daily total:

DAY 9:

    breakfast ....

    lunch ....

    dinner ....

    snacks ....

                                daily total:

DAY 10:

    breakfast ....

    lunch ....

    dinner ....

    snacks ....

                                  daily total:

DAY 11:

    breakfast ....

    lunch ....

    dinner ....

    snacks ....

                                  daily total:

DAY 12:

    breakfast ....

    lunch ....

    dinner ....

    snacks ....

                                  daily total:

DAY 13:

    breakfast ....

    lunch ....

    dinner ....

    snacks ....

                daily total:

DAY 14:

    breakfast ....

    lunch ....

    dinner ....

    snacks ....

                daily total:

height*	small frame	medium frame	large frame
4 ft. 10 in.	92–98	96–107	104–119
4 ft. 11 in.	94–101	98–110	106–122
5 ft. 0 in.	96–104	101–113	109–125
5 ft. 1 in.	99–107	104–116	112–128
5 ft. 2 in.	102–110	107–119	115–131
5 ft. 3 in.	105–113	110–122	118–134
5 ft. 4 in.	108–116	113–126	121–138
5 ft. 5 in.	111–119	116–130	125–142
5 ft. 6 in.	114–123	120–135	129–146
5 ft. 7 in.	118–127	124–139	133–150
5 ft. 8 in.	122–131	128–143	137–154
5 ft. 9 in.	126–135	132–147	141–158
5 ft. 10 in.	130–140	136–151	145–163
5 ft. 11 in.	134–144	140–155	149–168
6 ft. 0 in.	138–144	144–159	153–173

*With shoes—2-in. heels.

For women 18–25, subtract 1 pound for each year under 25.

height*	small frame	medium frame	large frame
5 ft. 2 in.	112–120	118–129	126–141
5 ft. 3 in.	115–123	121–133	129–144
5 ft. 4 in.	118–126	124–136	132–148
5 ft. 5 in.	121–129	127–139	135–152
5 ft. 6 in.	124–133	130–143	138–156
5 ft. 7 in.	128–137	134–147	142–161
5 ft. 8 in.	132–141	138–152	147–166
5 ft. 9 in.	136–145	142–156	151–170
5 ft. 10 in.	140–150	146–160	155–174
5 ft. 11 in.	144–154	150–165	159–179
6 ft. 0 in.	148–158	154–170	164–184
6 ft. 1 in.	152–162	158–175	168–189
6 ft. 2 in.	156–167	162–180	173–194
6 ft. 3 in.	160–171	167–185	178–199
6 ft. 4 in.	164–175	172–190	182–204

*With shoes—1-in. heels.
Prepared by the Metropolitan Life Insurance Co. from data of the Build and Blood Pressure Study, 1959, Society of Actuaries.

Dell BESTSELLERS